THE PELICAN SHAKESPEARE

GENERAL EDITOR ALFRED HARBAGE

THE HISTORY OF

TROILUS AND CRESSIDA

WILLIAM SHAKESPEARE

THE HISTORY OF TROILUS AND CRESSIDA

EDITED BY VIRGIL K. WHITAKER

PENGUIN BOOKS

BALTIMORE · MARYLAND

First published in *The Pelican Shakespeare* 1958
This revised edition first published 1970 by
Penguin Books Inc.
7110 Ambassador Road, Baltimore, Maryland 21207

Reprinted 1972

Printed in the United States of America

CONTENTS

PUBLISHER'S NOTE

Soon after the thirty-eight volumes forming *The Pelican Shakespeare* had been published, they were brought together in *The Complete Pelican Shakespeare*. The editorial revisions and new textual features are explained in detail in the General Editor's Preface to the one-volume edition. They have all been incorporated in the present volume. The following should be mentioned in particular:

The lines are not numbered in arbitrary units. Instead all lines are numbered which contain a word, phrase, or allusion explained in the glossarial notes. In the occasional instances where there is a long stretch of unannotated text, certain lines are numbered in italics to serve the conventional reference purpose.

The intrusive and often inaccurate place-headings inserted by early editors are omitted (as is becoming standard practise), but for the convenience of those who miss them, an indication of locale now appears as first item in the annotation of each scene.

In the interest of both elegance and utility, each speech-prefix is set in a separate line when the speaker's lines are in verse, except when these words form the second half of a pentameter line. Thus the verse form of the speech is kept visually intact, and turned-over lines are avoided. What is printed as verse and what is printed as prose has, in general, the authority of the original texts. Departures from the original texts in this regard have only the authority of editorial tradition and the judgment of the Pelican editors; and, in a few instances, are admittedly arbitrary.

SHAKESPEARE AND HIS STAGE

William Shakespeare was christened in Holy Trinity Church, Stratford-upon-Avon, April 26, 1564. His birth is traditionally assigned to April 23. He was the eldest of four boys and two girls who survived infancy in the family of John Shakespeare, glover and trader of Henley Street, and his wife Mary Arden, daughter of a small landowner of Wilmcote. In 1568 John was elected Bailiff (equivalent to Mayor) of Stratford, having already filled the minor municipal offices. The town maintained for the sons of the burgesses a free school, taught by a university graduate and offering preparation in Latin sufficient for university entrance; its early registers are lost, but there can be little doubt that Shakespeare received the formal part of his education in this school.

On November 27, 1582, a license was issued for the marriage of William Shakespeare (aged eighteen) and Ann Hathaway (aged twenty-six), and on May 26, 1583, their child Susanna was christened in Holy Trinity Church. The inference that the marriage was forced upon the youth is natural but not inevitable; betrothal was legally binding at the time, and was sometimes regarded as conferring conjugal rights. Two additional children of the marriage, the twins Hamnet and Judith, were christened on February 2, 1585. Meanwhile the prosperity of the elder Shakespeares had declined, and William was impelled to seek a career outside Stratford.

The tradition that he spent some time as a country

teacher is old but unverifiable. Because of the absence of records his early twenties are called the "lost years," and only one thing about them is certain – that at least some of these years were spent in winning a place in the acting profession. He may have begun as a provincial trouper, but by 1592 he was established in London and prominent enough to be attacked. In a pamphlet of that year, *Groats-worth of Wit*, the ailing Robert Greene complained of the neglect which university writers like himself had suffered from actors, one of whom was daring to set up as a playwright:

. . . an vpstart Crow, beautified with our feathers, that with his *Tygers hart wrapt in a Players hyde,* supposes he is as well able to bombast out a blanke verse as the best of you: and beeing an absolute *Iohannes fac totum*, is in his owne conceit the onely Shake-scene in a countrey.

The pun on his name, and the parody of his line "O tiger's heart wrapped in a woman's hide" (*3 Henry VI*), pointed clearly to Shakespeare. Some of his admirers protested, and Henry Chettle, the editor of Greene's pamphlet, saw fit to apologize:

. . . I am as sory as if the originall fault had beene my fault, because my selfe haue seene his demeanor no lesse ciuill than he excelent in the qualitie he professes: Besides, diuers of worship haue reported his vprightnes of dealing, which argues his honesty, and his facetious grace in writting, that approoues his Art. (Prefatory epistle, *Kind-Harts Dreame*)

The plague closed the London theatres for many months in 1592–94, denying the actors their livelihood. To this period belong Shakespeare's two narrative poems, *Venus and Adonis* and *The Rape of Lucrece*, both dedicated to the Earl of Southampton. No doubt the poet was rewarded with a gift of money as usual in such cases, but he did no further dedicating and we have no reliable information on whether Southampton, or anyone else, became his regular patron. His sonnets, first mentioned in 1598 and published without his consent in 1609, are intimate without being

8

explicitly autobiographical. They seem to commemorate the poet's friendship with an idealized youth, rivalry with a more favored poet, and love affair with a dark mistress; and his bitterness when the mistress betrays him in conjunction with the friend; but it is difficult to decide precisely what the "story" is, impossible to decide whether it is fictional or true. The true distinction of the sonnets, at least of those not purely conventional, rests in the universality of the thoughts and moods they express, and in their poignancy and beauty.

In 1594 was formed the theatrical company known until 1603 as the Lord Chamberlain's men, thereafter as the King's men. Its original membership included, besides Shakespeare, the beloved clown Will Kempe and the famous actor Richard Burbage. The company acted in various London theatres and even toured the provinces, but it is chiefly associated in our minds with the Globe Theatre built on the south bank of the Thames in 1599. Shakespeare was an actor and joint owner of this company (and its Globe) through the remainder of his creative years. His plays, written at the average rate of two a year, together with Burbage's acting won it its place of leadership among the London companies.

Individual plays began to appear in print, in editions both honest and piratical, and the publishers became increasingly aware of the value of Shakespeare's name on the title pages. As early as 1598 he was hailed as the leading English dramatist in the *Palladis Tamia* of Francis Meres:

As *Plautus* and *Seneca* are accounted the best for Comedy and Tragedy among the Latines, so *Shakespeare* among the English is the most excellent in both kinds for the stage: for Comedy, witnes his *Gentlemen of Verona*, his *Errors*, his *Loue labors lost*, his *Loue labours wonne* [at one time in print but no longer extant, at least under this title], his *Midsummers night dream*, & his *Merchant of Venice*; for Tragedy, his *Richard the 2*, *Richard the 3*, *Henry the 4*, *King Iohn*, *Titus Andronicus*, and his *Romeo and Iuliet*.

The note is valuable both in indicating Shakespeare's prestige and in helping us to establish a chronology. In the second half of his writing career, history plays gave place to the great tragedies; and farces and light comedies gave place to the problem plays and symbolic romances. In 1623, seven years after his death, his former fellow-actors, John Heminge and Henry Condell, cooperated with a group of London printers in bringing out his plays in collected form. The volume is generally known as the First Folio.

Shakespeare had never severed his relations with Stratford. His wife and children may sometimes have shared his London lodgings, but their home was Stratford. His son Hamnet was buried there in 1596, and his daughters Susanna and Judith were married there in 1607 and 1616 respectively. (His father, for whom he had secured a coat of arms and thus the privilege of writing himself gentleman, died in 1601, his mother in 1608.) His considerable earnings in London, as actor-sharer, part owner of the Globe, and playwright, were invested chiefly in Stratford property. In 1597 he purchased for £60 New Place, one of the two most imposing residences in the town. A number of other business transactions, as well as minor episodes in his career, have left documentary records. By 1611 he was in a position to retire, and he seems gradually to have withdrawn from theatrical activity in order to live in Stratford. In March, 1616, he made a will, leaving token bequests to Burbage, Heminge, and Condell, but the bulk of his estate to his family. The most famous feature of the will, the bequest of the second-best bed to his wife, reveals nothing about Shakespeare's marriage; the quaintness of the provision seems commonplace to those familiar with ancient testaments. Shakespeare died April 23, 1616, and was buried in the Stratford church where he had been christened. Within seven years a monument was erected to his memory on the north wall of the chancel. Its portrait bust and the Droeshout engraving on the title page of the First Folio provide the only likenesses with an established claim to authenticity. The best verbal vignette was written by his rival Ben Jonson, the more impressive for being imbedded in a context mainly critical:

... I loved the man, and doe honour his memory (on this side idolatry) as much as any. Hee was indeed honest, and of an open and free nature: had an excellent Phantsie, brave notions, and gentle expressions.... (*Timber or Discoveries*, ca. 1623-30)

*

The reader of Shakespeare's plays is aided by a general knowledge of the way in which they were staged. The King's men acquired a roofed and artificially lighted theatre only toward the close of Shakespeare's career, and then only for winter use. Nearly all his plays were designed for performance in such structures as the Globe – a three-tiered amphitheatre with a large rectangular platform extending to the center of its yard. The plays were staged by daylight, by large casts brilliantly costumed, but with only a minimum of properties, without scenery, and quite possibly without intermissions. There was a rear stage gallery for action "above," and a curtained rear recess for "discoveries" and other special effects, but by far the major portion of any play was enacted upon the projecting platform, with episode following episode in swift succession, and with shifts of time and place signaled the audience only by the momentary clearing of the stage between the episodes. Information about the identity of the characters and, when necessary, about the time and place of the action was incorporated in the dialogue. No place-headings have been inserted in the present editions; these are apt to obscure the original fluidity of structure, with the emphasis upon action and speech rather than scenic background. (Indications of place are supplied in the footnotes.) The acting, including that of the youthful apprentices to the profession who performed the parts of women, was highly skillful, with a premium placed upon grace of gesture and beauty of diction. The audiences, a cross section of the general public, commonly numbered a thousand, sometimes more than two thousand. Judged by the type of plays they applauded, these audiences were not only large but also perceptive.

THE TEXTS OF THE PLAYS

About half of Shakespeare's plays appeared in print for the first time in the folio volume of 1623. The others had been published individually, usually in quarto volumes, during his lifetime or in the six years following his death. The copy used by the printers of the quartos varied greatly in merit, sometimes representing Shakespeare's true text, sometimes only a debased version of that text. The copy used by the printers of the folio also varied in merit, but was chosen with care. Since it consisted of the best available manuscripts, or the more acceptable quartos (although frequently in editions other than the first), or of quartos corrected by reference to manuscripts, we have good or reasonably good texts of most of the thirty-seven plays.

In the present series, the plays have been newly edited from quarto or folio texts, depending, when a choice offered, upon which is now regarded by bibliographical specialists as the more authoritative. The ideal has been to reproduce the chosen texts with as few alterations as possible, beyond occasional relineation, expansion of abbreviations, and modernization of punctuation and spelling. Emendation is held to a minimum, and such material as has been added, in the way of stage directions and lines supplied by an alternative text, has been enclosed in square brackets.

None of the plays printed in Shakespeare's lifetime were divided into acts and scenes, and the inference is that the author's own manuscripts were not so divided. In the folio collection, some of the plays remained undivided, some were divided into acts, and some were divided into acts and scenes. During the eighteenth century all of the plays were divided into acts and scenes, and in the Cambridge edition of the mid-nineteenth century, from which the influential Globe text derived, this division was more or less regularized and the lines were numbered. Many useful works of reference employ the act–scene–line apparatus thus established.

Since this act–scene division is obviously convenient, but is of very dubious authority so far as Shakespeare's own structural principles are concerned, or the original manner of staging his plays, a problem is presented to modern editors. In the present series the act–scene division is retained marginally, and may be viewed as a reference aid like the line numbering. A star marks the points of division when these points have been determined by a cleared stage indicating a shift of time and place in the action of the play, or when no harm results from the editorial assumption that there is such a shift. However, at those points where the established division is clearly misleading – that is, where continuous action has been split up into separate "scenes" – the star is omitted and the distortion corrected. This mechanical expedient seemed the best means of combining utility and accuracy.

THE GENERAL EDITOR

INTRODUCTION

Troilus and Cressida remains an enigma. Complications surrounded its first publication; our only clues to its first performance are a puzzle; the customary dramatic categories will neither explain nor include it; and its fascination for the intellect cannot conceal its defects as art.

On February 7, 1603, there was entered in the Stationers' Register for copyright "The booke of Troilus and Cresseda as yt is acted by my lord Chamberlens men." There is a second entry in 1609 for different publishers, whose quarto edition shortly appeared under the title "The Historie of Troylus and Cresseida. As it was acted by the Kings Maiesties seruants at the Globe. Written by William Shakespeare." But the same text was immediately reissued with the original title page cut away and two new leaves substituted. The first bore a different title: "The Famous Historie of Troylus and Cresseid. Excellently expressing the beginning of their loues, with the conceited wooing of Pandarus Prince of Licia. Written by William Shakespeare." The second leaf contained the preface, "A Never Writer, to an Ever Reader. News," which heads the present edition. In conjunction with the new title, this preface looks like an attempt to urge as a selling point that the play had never been "clapper-clawed with the palms of the vulgar" – that is, had never been performed in the public theatre. The subsequent sentences also imply that the play, having displeased the witless, is now being offered to its proper patrons, the witty.

14

Still further complications ensued when the first folio was being prepared. Three pages of the play were actually printed for inclusion among the tragedies after *Romeo and Juliet*. Then, presumably because of copyright difficulties, these were withdrawn and *Timon of Athens* was substituted. Finally the play was printed without pagination, too late for inclusion in the preliminary list of plays, and placed between the histories and the tragedies in the complete folio.

The facts just related provide our best clues to the date and performance of the play. Most critics date it about 1602 on the basis of style and allusions in the text, although dissenters have placed it in the late 1590's. One may perhaps conjecture that, shortly before February 7, 1603, it was performed by Shakespeare's company, then the Lord Chamberlain's Men, but for a special audience rather than before the "vulgar" in the Globe Theatre. The character of the play suggests performance before one of the Inns of Court, where wit might be found, if anywhere. It was not unusual for plays to be performed before special audiences at the time, but it must be conceded that it was quite unusual for plays to be especially written for such performances.

Hence we are dealing here not with an established fact, as is sometimes assumed, but with a hypothesis only, although it comes as near as any to explaining the peculiar characteristics of *Troilus and Cressida* : the play is a unique combination of learned subject matter, all-inclusive satire, and something close to smut ; and it is neither comedy nor tragedy – nor, in fact, well-constructed drama. A subject with the most respectable literary antecedents has been treated disrespectfully enough to appeal to the sophisticated and cynical.

Of the two plot-threads of the play, the story of Troilus and Cressida is drawn from Chaucer's *Troilus and Criseyde*. In the background, though little used in the play, lurks Robert Henryson's *Testament of Cresseid*, a sequel in which

Cresseid becomes a leper and a beggar. For the military episodes Shakespeare drew upon Caxton's *Recuyell of the Historyes of Troye*, upon Homer in Chapman's translation, and, for such details as the romantic motive of Hector's challenge, upon his own familiarity with tales of chivalry. But the knightly trappings of the Trojan War are thoroughly in accord with the medieval versions of the Troy story that lay behind all his sources but Homer. The subject was dramatically timely. In 1599 Dekker and Chettle had written a play on Troilus and Cressida for the Admiral's Men, a rival company; and Chapman's *Sir Giles Goosecap*, a comedy contemporary with Shakespeare's play, adapted some of the story elements to English characters in an English setting. Shakespeare, too, may have been trying to give the story a novel treatment, partly by his dissection of the moral issues involved in the war. For this ethical analysis he may have found precedent in Robert Greene's *Euphues His Censure to Philautus* (1587).

Either the classical subject matter or a learned audience may account for the style of the play. Passages in *Troilus and Cressida* come closer than anything else in Shakespeare to the epic style that Milton developed, on the precedent of Latin epic, for *Paradise Lost*. This is true not only of the Latinate diction but also of the figurative language, extreme even by Elizabethan standards and particularly prone to such devices as personification, hyperbole, or substituting an abstraction for a plural noun:

> But let the ruffian Boreas once enrage
> The gentle Thetis, and anon behold
> The strong-ribbed bark through liquid mountains cut.
> (I, iii, 38–40)

> The specialty of rule hath been neglected.   (I, iii, 78)

Either the audience or Shakespeare's own preoccupation with philosophic ideas must account for the long passages in the two council scenes that make the play almost a sum-mary of Shakespeare's cosmology and ethics. These will be discussed below.

If Shakespeare finds a grand style appropriate to his retelling of a great love story and the greatest of all war stories, his treatment nevertheless results in a total deflation of both romance and glory. Troilus is an estimable young man, but he is an erotic gourmet nonetheless :

> I am giddy ; expectation whirls me round.
> Th' imaginary relish is so sweet
> That it enchants my sense. What will it be
> When that the wat'ry palates taste indeed
> Love's thrice-repurèd nectar ? Death, I fear me,
> Sounding destruction, or some joy too fine,
> Too subtle, potent, tuned too sharp in sweetness
> For the capacity of my ruder powers.   (III, ii, 16–23)

This is human enough, but it is not romantic love. As to Cressida, if we have any doubts after her exchange of wit with Pandarus at the end of the second scene, they are immediately dispelled by her own words. She is a practiced "daughter of the game," as Ulysses later calls her. She sums herself up :

> Ah, poor our sex ! this fault in us I find,
> The error of our eye directs our mind.
> What error leads must err. O, then conclude
> Minds swayed by eyes are full of turpitude.
>   (V, ii, 105–08)

When Troilus discovers his mistake in supposing that the woman he has seduced is proof against other men, he is pathetic in his grief, but he is not tragic.

The Trojan War is even more thoroughly deflated. Thersites sums the matter up in his scurrilous way : "All the argument is a whore and a cuckold, a good quarrel to draw emulous factions and bleed to death upon" (II, iii, 68–70). Helen's own character and the atmosphere that surrounds her are perfectly suggested by Pandarus' long

scene with her, and particularly by the tone of the song
that concludes it (III, i). Diomedes gets down to cases :

> For every false drop in her bawdy veins
> A Grecian's life hath sunk ; for every scruple
> Of her contaminated carrion weight
> A Troyan hath been slain. Since she could speak,
> She hath not given so many good words breath
> As for her Greeks and Troyans suff'red death.
>
> (IV, i, 69–74)

The Greeks, therefore, are trying to recover what is not
worth fighting for ; but they quarrel like spoiled and selfish
children, and Achilles, their hero, is a vainglorious muscle-
man. He pouts in his tent with his favorite and, in defiance
of Homer's account, has his Myrmidons ambush Hector,
who is unarmed. He is, in short, a bully and a coward. The
Trojans are very different but equally flawed. They know
their cause is wrong. Hector proves all too clearly that

> these moral laws
> Of nature and of nations speak aloud
> To have her [Helen] back returned.   (II, ii, 184–86)

He knows that Troilus, in arguing for keeping her, is
driven by passion as against judgment :

> Or is your blood
> So madly hot that no discourse of reason,
> Nor fear of bad success in a bad cause,
> Can qualify the same ?   (II, ii, 115–18)

But, after enunciating the soundest moral principles, he
reverses himself and concludes :

> Hector's opinion
> Is this in way of truth ; yet ne'ertheless,
> My spritely brethren, I propend to you
> In resolution to keep Helen still ;
> For 'tis a cause that hath no mean dependence
> Upon our joint and several dignities.
>
> (II, ii, 188–93)

As a fighter, he is as reckless in his chivalry as Achilles is cowardly. He is playing foolishly in a foolish war. The rational norm of bravery is not in either man. In this play (though nowhere else in Shakespeare) war is what it is in much modern fiction – a bloody mess from which no one emerges with glory or even integrity.

The intention of the play is therefore ambiguous. Apparently it puzzled Shakespeare's contemporaries. The second entry in the Stationers' Register and the quarto title pages call it a history – that is, a dramatic narrative of historical events which is not definitely tragedy. The folio editors intended to place it among the tragedies and called it "The Tragedie of Troylus and Cressida." Elizabethan literary theory restricted comedy to non-historical subject matter. But the play is simply not tragedy, even though it ends with the death of Troilus' illusions and of Hector himself. Its subject matter, unlike its style, is never heroic, and in Thersites it descends to obscene raillery. The war plot has only the loosest narrative organization, and the two great council scenes have no dramatic function at all proportionate to the pains that Shakespeare lavished upon them. Perhaps the best hypothesis is that he tried to adapt the well-known story to the satiric mood then in fashion in the theatre and to make it especially palatable to a learned and sophisticated audience by seasoning it with large, unassimilated chunks of philosophy and a liberal sprinkling of innuendo or even outright scurrility. But, if so, his attempt to turn what was for his audience a great historical theme into comical satire was unique in the Elizabethan theatre.

What has the play to offer the modern reader? The answer, despite what precedes, is that it is Shakespeare's own key to his greatest plays and that it is a powerful, if unconventional, mirror of human nature.

Shakespeare, like most of his contemporaries, believed that God the Creator had imposed upon all nature a universal and hierarchical order, in accordance with which all things performed their part in achieving His ultimate purposes. This order resulted from the obedience of all creation to laws that governed not only the physical universe but also social and political institutions and man the individual. As a rational being and the highest of created things on earth, man shared with God and the angels the possession of free will. He was free to live rationally – that is, to obey the commands of God and conform to the laws of nature. But he was also free to violate "the moral laws of nature and of nations" and, by so doing, to bring suffering upon himself and disruption to the social and even cosmic order of which he was a part. This view is present throughout the plays; it is fundamental to the great tragedies. Shakespeare's concept of universal order is stated fully and explicitly in Ulysses' great speech to the Greek council (I, iii, 75–137). His explanation of human disorder is summarized, more succinctly, in Hector's parallel argument to the Trojan council in the next act (II, ii, 163–93). The decision of the council and of Hector himself is, moreover, an example of "those raging appetites" that overcome the reason and will, and lead men to corrupt the law of nature. And the play is filled with short passages that echo or clarify the same system of ideas, as the psychology and ethics of love and war are analyzed explicitly and fully. In the tragedies Shakespeare presents in action what here he explains in theoretical terms. Always, as in *Othello* and *Macbeth*, we see man's will "benumbed" in sin; in *Macbeth* and *King Lear* we also see "what discord follows" the destruction of "degree," and in *King Lear* the "appetite" that disrupts nature

> Must make perforce an universal prey
> And last eat up himself. (I, iii, 123–24)

So evil becomes self-destructive, and order is restored to a suffering world. In short, the lover of Shakespeare must know *Troilus and Cressida* thoroughly, or he does not know Shakespeare at all.

But *Troilus and Cressida* itself portrays a very different world from that of tragedy, the world of all-too-human nature. The satire is sharp, but it is justified. The modern reader of the play does not need to be told that what passes for love is often lust, and that what motivates much patriotism has nothing to do with love of country. Modern literature has made these points in wearisome detail. But Shakespeare has intensified and clarified even this aspect of human nature with all the matchless resources of his imagination. His eye has roved from the councils of the mighty to the backbiting of their hangers-on. Modern fiction has done much better, moreover, at giving us Cressidas, or a Pandarus and Thersites, than at showing us a Hector betraying his intellect under pressure of the moment or a Ulysses expending his wisdom on an intrigue to end a petty broil. And Shakespeare has summarized these insights in unforgettable lines of verse. *Troilus and Cressida* is certainly not his greatest play, but it is in some respects his most modern. We may not like its people, but they are with us everywhere. Shakespeare often tells us what we can be or should be. Here he tells us what, unfortunately, we all too often are.

Stanford University   VIRGIL K. WHITAKER

NOTE ON THE TEXT

The present edition is based on the quarto of 1609, which is believed to have been printed from a private transcript of Shakespeare's own draft made by himself or a scribe. The folio text was printed from the quarto, perhaps collated with the original draft after it had been prepared for performance. A few brief passages supplied by the folio have been included in square brackets, and a number of readings from the folio have been adopted at points where the text of the quarto seems corrupt or obviously inferior.

These, and the limited number of emendations, are listed in the Appendix. The stage directions are those of the quarto, with bracketed additions and amplifications suggested usually by the folio. Both the quarto and folio are without act–scene divisions, and those of the later editors have been supplied marginally.

THE HISTORY OF
TROILUS AND
CRESSIDA

A NEVER WRITER,
TO AN EVER READER.
NEWS.

Eternal reader, you have here a new play, never staled
with the stage, never clapper-clawed with the palms of the
vulgar, and yet passing full of the palm comical; for it is a
birth of your brain that never undertook anything comical
vainly. And were but the vain names of comedies changed
for the titles of commodities, or of plays for pleas, you
should see all those grand censors, that now style them such
vanities, flock to them for the main grace of their gravities,
especially this author's comedies, that are so framed to the
10 life that they serve for the most common commentaries of
all the actions of our lives, showing such a dexterity and
power of wit that the most displeased with plays are pleased
with his comedies. And all such dull and heavy-witted
worldlings as were never capable of the wit of a comedy,
coming by report of them to his representations, have found
that wit there that they never found in themselves and have
parted better witted than they came, feeling an edge of wit
set upon them more than ever they dreamed they had brain
to grind it on. So much and such savored salt of wit is in his
comedies that they seem, for their height of pleasure, to be
21 born in that sea that brought forth Venus. Amongst all there
is none more witty than this: and had I time I would com-
ment upon it, though I know it needs not, for so much as
24 will make you think your testern well bestowed, but for so

Preface   **21** *Venus* (the Latin goddess was identified with the Greek
Aphrodite, who sprang from the sea foam)   **24** *testern* sixpence

much worth as even poor I know to be stuffed in it. It deserves such a labor as well as the best comedy in Terence or Plautus. And believe this, that when he is gone and his comedies out of sale, you will scramble for them and set up a new English Inquisition. Take this for a warning, and at the peril of your pleasure's loss, and judgment's, refuse not, nor like this the less for not being sullied with the smoky breath of the multitude ; but thank fortune for the 'scape it hath made amongst you, since by the grand possessors' 33 wills I believe you should have prayed for them rather than been prayed. And so I leave all such to be prayed for, for the state of their wits' healths, that will not praise it. Vale.

33 grand possessors (the actor-sharers of the King's Men, who apparently were trying to prevent the publication of their plays)

[NAMES OF THE ACTORS

Priam, *King of Troy*
Hector ⎫
Troilus ⎪
Paris ⎬ *his sons*
Deiphobus ⎪
Helenus ⎭
Margarelon, *a bastard son of Priam*
Aeneas ⎫
Antenor ⎬ *Trojan commanders*
Calchas, *a Trojan priest, taking part with the Greeks*
Pandarus, *uncle to Cressida*
Agamemnon, *the Greek general*
Menelaus, *his brother*
Achilles ⎫
Ajax ⎬ *Greek commanders*
Ulysses ⎫
Nestor ⎪
Diomedes ⎬ *Greek commanders*
Patroclus ⎭
Thersites, *a deformed and scurrilous Greek*
Alexander, *servant to Cressida*
Servant to Troilus
Servant to Paris
Servant to Diomedes
Helen, *wife to Menelaus*
Andromache, *wife to Hector*
Cassandra, *daughter to Priam ; a prophetess*
Cressida, *daughter to Calchas*
Trojan and Greek Soldiers and Attendants

Scene : *Troy, and the Greek Camp before it*]

THE HISTORY OF
TROILUS AND
CRESSIDA

[THE PROLOGUE

In Troy there lies the scene. From isles of Greece
The princes orgulous, their high blood chafed,   2
Have to the port of Athens sent their ships,
Fraught with the ministers and instruments
Of cruel war. Sixty and nine, that wore
Their crownets regal, from th' Athenian bay
Put forth toward Phrygia ; and their vow is made   7
To ransack Troy, within whose strong immures   8
The ravished Helen, Menelaus' queen,
With wanton Paris sleeps ; and that's the quarrel.
To Tenedos they come,
And the deep-drawing barks do there disgorge
Their warlike fraughtage. Now on Dardan plains   13
The fresh and yet unbruisèd Greeks do pitch
Their brave pavilions. Priam's six-gated city,
Dardan, and Timbria, Helias, Chetas, Troien,   16
And Antenonidus, with massy staples
And corresponsive and fulfilling bolts,   18
Sperr up the sons of Troy.   19
Now expectation, tickling skittish spirits,

Pro. 2 *orgulous* proud 7 *Phrygia* western Asia Minor 8 *immures* walls
13 *fraughtage* cargo, i.e. warriors; *Dardan* Trojan, Dardanus being a
mythical ancestor 16–17 *Dardan . . . Antenonidus* (i.e. Antenorides)
names of the gates 18 *fulfilling* filling full, i.e. tightly 19 *Sperr* shut

27

On one and other side, Troyan and Greek,
Sets all on hazard. And hither am I come,

23 A prologue armed, but not in confidence
24 Of author's pen or actor's voice, but suited
25 In like conditions as our argument,
To tell you, fair beholders, that our play

27 Leaps o'er the vaunt and firstlings of those broils,
Beginning in the middle, starting thence away
To what may be digested in a play.
Like or find fault; do as your pleasures are:
Now good or bad, 'tis but the chance of war.]

I, i   *Enter Pandarus and Troilus.*

TROILUS

1   Call here my varlet, I'll unarm again.
Why should I war without the walls of Troy
That find such cruel battle here within?
Each Troyan that is master of his heart,
Let him to field; Troilus, alas, hath none.

PANDARUS

6   Will this gear ne'er be mended?

TROILUS

7   The Greeks are strong, and skillful to their strength,
Fierce to their skill, and to their fierceness valiant;
But I am weaker than a woman's tear,

10   Tamer than sleep, fonder than ignorance,
Less valiant than the virgin in the night,
And skilless as unpractised infancy.

PANDARUS Well, I have told you enough of this. For my
part, I'll not meddle nor make no farther. He that will
have a cake out of the wheat must tarry the grinding.

TROILUS Have I not tarried?

23 *armed* in armor   24 *suited* dressed   25 *argument* theme, subject   27
vaunt first part
I, i Before the palace of Priam in Troy   1 *varlet* servant   6 *gear* business
7 *to* in addition to   10 *fonder* more foolish

28

PANDARUS Ay, the grinding; but you must tarry the
bolting.
17

TROILUS Have I not tarried?

PANDARUS Ay, the bolting; but you must tarry the
leavening.

TROILUS Still have I tarried.

PANDARUS Ay, to the leavening; but here's yet in the
word 'hereafter' the kneading, the making of the cake,
the heating of the oven, and the baking; nay, you must
stay the cooling too, or you may chance to burn your lips.

TROILUS
Patience herself, what goddess e'er she be,
Doth lesser blench at suff'rance than I do.
26
At Priam's royal table do I sit,
And when fair Cressid comes into my thoughts –
So, traitor, then she comes when she is thence.
29

PANDARUS Well, she looked yesternight fairer than ever
I saw her look, or any woman else.

TROILUS
I was about to tell thee, when my heart,
As wedgèd with a sigh, would rive in twain,
33
Lest Hector or my father should perceive me:
I have, as when the sun doth light a-scorn,
35
Buried this sigh in wrinkle of a smile;
But sorrow, that is couched in seeming gladness,
Is like that mirth fate turns to sudden sadness.

PANDARUS An her hair were not somewhat darker than
39
Helen's – well, go to – there were no more comparison
between the women: but, for my part, she is my kins-
woman; I would not, as they term it, praise her, but I
would somebody had heard her talk yesterday, as I did.
I will not dispraise your sister Cassandra's wit, but –

TROILUS
O Pandarus! I tell thee, Pandarus –

17 *bolting* sifting   26 *blench* flinch   29 *traitor* (a rebuke for implying that
she may ever be absent)   33 *rive* split   35 *a-scorn* grudgingly (?)   39 *An* if

When I do tell thee, there my hopes lie drowned,
Reply not in how many fathoms deep
They lie indrenched. I tell thee I am mad
In Cressid's love; thou answer'st she is fair;
Pour'st in the open ulcer of my heart
Her eyes, her hair, her cheek, her gait, her voice;
52   Handlest in thy discourse, O, that her hand,
In whose comparison all whites are ink,
Writing their own reproach; to whose soft seizure
55   The cygnet's down is harsh, and spirit of sense
Hard as the palm of ploughman. This thou tell'st me,
As true thou tell'st me, when I say I love her;
But, saying thus, instead of oil and balm,
Thou lay'st in every gash that love hath given me
The knife that made it.

PANDARUS I speak no more than truth.

TROILUS Thou dost not speak so much.

PANDARUS Faith, I'll not meddle in it. Let her be as she
is. If she be fair, 'tis the better for her; an she be not, she
65   has the mends in her own hands.

TROILUS Good Pandarus, how now, Pandarus?

PANDARUS I have had my labor for my travail; ill-
thought-on of her, and ill-thought-on of you; gone between and between, but small thanks for my labor.

TROILUS What, art thou angry, Pandarus? what, with
me?

PANDARUS Because she's kin to me, therefore she's not so
72   fair as Helen. An she were not kin to me, she would be as
fair on Friday as Helen is on Sunday. But what care I?
74   I care not an she were a blackamoor; 'tis all one to me.

TROILUS Say I she is not fair?

---

52 *that her hand* that hand of hers   **55** *cygnet's* young swan's; *spirit* a very
thin bodily substance that was believed to transmit sense impressions
through the nerves   **65** *mends* remedies, i.e. cosmetics   **72–73** *as fair* . . .
Sunday as fair in ordinary clothes as Helen in her Sunday best   **74** *blackamoor* Negro

PANDARUS I do not care whether you do or no. She's a
   fool to stay behind her father. Let her to the Greeks, and 77
   so I'll tell her the next time I see her. For my part, I'll
   meddle nor make no more i' th' matter.
TROILUS Pandarus—
PANDARUS Not I.
TROILUS Sweet Pandarus—
PANDARUS Pray you, speak no more to me. I will leave all
   as I found it, and there an end.   *Exit. Sound alarum.* 84
TROILUS
   Peace, you ungracious clamors! Peace, rude sounds!
   Fools on both sides! Helen must needs be fair,
   When with your blood you daily paint her thus.
   I cannot fight upon this argument;   88
   It is too starved a subject for my sword.
   But Pandarus—O gods, how do you plague me!
   I cannot come to Cressid but by Pandar;
   And he's as tetchy to be wooed to woo   92
   As she is stubborn, chaste, against all suit.
   Tell me, Apollo, for thy Daphne's love,   94
   What Cressid is, what Pandar, and what we.
   Her bed is India; there she lies, a pearl.
   Between our Ilium and where she resides   97
   Let it be called the wild and wand'ring flood,
   Ourself the merchant, and this sailing Pandar
   Our doubtful hope, our convoy and our bark.
        Alarum. Enter Aeneas.
AENEAS
   How now, Prince Troilus, wherefore not afield?
TROILUS
   Because not there. This woman's answer sorts,
   For womanish it is to be from thence.

---

77 *father* Calchas, a seer who anticipated the Trojan defeat and deserted
to the Greeks 84 **s.d.** *alarum* signal to arms 88 *argument* subject of
contention 92 *tetchy* fretful 94 *Daphne* a nymph beloved of Apollo,
who was changed into a bay tree to escape his pursuit 97 *Ilium* here,
Priam's palace

What news, Aeneas, from the field to-day?

AENEAS
That Paris is returnèd home, and hurt.

TROILUS
By whom, Aeneas?

AENEAS   Troilus, by Menelaus.

TROILUS
Let Paris bleed; 'tis but a scar to scorn.
108 Paris is gored with Menelaus' horn.
          Alarum.

AENEAS
Hark what good sport is out of town to-day!

TROILUS
Better at home, if 'would I might' were 'may.'
But to the sport abroad. Are you bound thither?

AENEAS
In all swift haste.

TROILUS   Come, go we then together.   *Exeunt*.

*

I, ii   *Enter Cressida and [Alexander,] her man.*

CRESSIDA
Who were those went by?

MAN   Queen Hecuba and Helen.

CRESSIDA
And whither go they?

MAN   Up to the eastern tower,
Whose height commands as subject all the vale,
To see the battle. Hector, whose patience
Is as a virtue fixed, to-day was moved.
He chid Andromache, and struck his armorer,
7   And, like as there were husbandry in war,

---

108 *horn* (symbol of a cuckold, a man whose wife had been unfaithful.
Paris had stolen Helen from Menelaus.)
I, ii Before the house of Cressida   7 *husbandry* thrift

Before the sun rose he was harnessed light,   8
And to the field goes he, where every flower
Did, as a prophet, weep what it foresaw
In Hector's wrath.

CRESSIDA   What was his cause of anger?

MAN
The noise goes, this: there is among the Greeks
A lord of Troyan blood, nephew to Hector;
They call him Ajax.

CRESSIDA   Good; and what of him?

MAN
They say he is a very man per se
And stands alone.

CRESSIDA So do all men unless they are drunk, sick, or
have no legs.

MAN This man, lady, hath robbed many beasts of their particular additions: he is as valiant as the lion, churlish as   20
the bear, slow as the elephant; a man into whom nature
hath so crowded humors that his valor is crushed into   22
folly, his folly sauced with discretion. There is no man
hath a virtue that he hath not a glimpse of, nor any man   24
an attaint but he carries some stain of it. He is melan-   25
choly without cause and merry against the hair. He hath   26
the joints of everything, but everything so out of joint
that he is a gouty Briareus, many hands and no use, or   28
purblind Argus, all eyes and no sight.   29

CRESSIDA But how should this man that makes me smile
make Hector angry?

MAN They say he yesterday coped Hector in the battle   32
and struck him down, the disdain and shame whereof
hath ever since kept Hector fasting and waking.

---

8 *harnessed* in armor   20 *additions* indications of rank or distinction added
to a man's name   22 *humors* bodily fluids the excess of which caused
emotional disorders   24 *glimpse* spark   25 *attaint* stain on honor   26 *hair*
natural tendency   28 *Briareus* a hundred-handed giant   29 *Argus* a herds-
man who had eyes all over his body   32 *coped* came to blows with

33

[Enter Pandarus.]

CRESSIDA Who comes here?

MAN Madam, your uncle Pandarus.

CRESSIDA Hector's a gallant man.

MAN As may be in the world, lady.

PANDARUS What's that? What's that?

CRESSIDA Good morrow, uncle Pandarus.

41 PANDARUS Good morrow, cousin Cressid. What do you talk of? Good morrow, Alexander. How do you, cousin? When were you at Ilium?

CRESSIDA This morning, uncle.

PANDARUS What were you talking of when I came? Was Hector armed and gone ere ye came to Ilium? Helen was not up, was she?

CRESSIDA Hector was gone, but Helen was not up.

PANDARUS E'en so, Hector was stirring early.

CRESSIDA That were we talking of, and of his anger.

PANDARUS Was he angry?

52 CRESSIDA So he says here.

PANDARUS True, he was so. I know the cause too. He'll lay about him to-day, I can tell them that; and there's Troilus will not come far behind him. Let them take heed of Troilus, I can tell them that too.

CRESSIDA What, is he angry too?

PANDARUS Who, Troilus? Troilus is the better man of the two.

CRESSIDA O Jupiter! there's no comparison.

PANDARUS What, not between Troilus and Hector? Do you know a man if you see him?

CRESSIDA Ay, if I ever saw him before and knew him.

PANDARUS Well, I say Troilus is Troilus.

CRESSIDA Then you say as I say, for I am sure he is not Hector.

67 PANDARUS No, nor Hector is not Troilus in some degrees.

CRESSIDA 'Tis just to each of them; he is himself.

41 *cousin* i.e. niece   52 *he* i.e. Alexander   67 *in some degrees* by some distance

34

PANDARUS Himself? Alas, poor Troilus, I would he were. 69
CRESSIDA So he is.
PANDARUS Condition, I had gone barefoot to India. 71
CRESSIDA He is not Hector.
PANDARUS Himself? no, he's not himself. Would 'a were himself! Well, the gods are above; time must friend or end. Well, Troilus, well, I would my heart were in her body. No, Hector is not a better man than Troilus.
CRESSIDA Excuse me.
PANDARUS He is elder.
CRESSIDA Pardon me, pardon me.
PANDARUS Th' other's not come to't; you shall tell me 80
another tale when th' other's come to't. Hector shall not have his wit this year. 82
CRESSIDA He shall not need it if he have his own.
PANDARUS Nor his qualities.
CRESSIDA No matter.
PANDARUS Nor his beauty.
CRESSIDA 'Twould not become him; his own's better.
PANDARUS You have no judgment, niece. Helen herself swore th' other day that Troilus, for a brown favor – for 89
so 'tis, I must confess, not brown neither –
CRESSIDA No, but brown.
PANDARUS Faith, to say truth, brown and not brown.
CRESSIDA To say the truth, true and not true.
PANDARUS She praised his complexion above Paris.
CRESSIDA Why, Paris hath color enough.
PANDARUS So he has.
CRESSIDA Then Troilus should have too much. If she praised him above, his complexion is higher than his. He having color enough, and the other higher, is too flaming a praise for a good complexion. I had as lief Helen's golden tongue had commended Troilus for a copper nose.

69 *I would he were* i.e. himself, and not in love 71 *Condition . . . India* even though it meant my going barefoot to India 80 *come to't* come to manhood 82 *wit* intelligence 89 *favor* complexion

PANDARUS I swear to you, I think Helen loves him better than Paris.

104 CRESSIDA Then she's a merry Greek indeed.

PANDARUS Nay, I am sure she does. She came to him th'
106 other day into the compassed window, and, you know, he has not past three or four hairs on his chin –

CRESSIDA Indeed, a tapster's arithmetic may soon bring his particulars therein to a total.

PANDARUS Why, he is very young; and yet will he, within three pound, lift as much as his brother Hector.

112 CRESSIDA Is he so young a man, and so old a lifter?

PANDARUS But to prove to you that Helen loves him, she came and puts me her white hand to his cloven chin –

CRESSIDA Juno have mercy! how came it cloven?

PANDARUS Why, you know 'tis dimpled. I think his smiling becomes him better than any man in all Phrygia.

CRESSIDA O, he smiles valiantly.

PANDARUS Does he not?

CRESSIDA O, yes, an 'twere a cloud in autumn.

PANDARUS Why, go to then. But to prove to you that Helen loves Troilus –

CRESSIDA Troilus will stand to the proof, if you'll prove it so.

PANDARUS Troilus? Why, he esteems her no more than
125 I esteem an addle egg.

CRESSIDA If you love an addle egg as well as you love an idle head, you would eat chickens i' th' shell.

PANDARUS I cannot choose but laugh to think how she tickled his chin. Indeed, she has a marvell's white hand, I must needs confess.

131 CRESSIDA Without the rack.

PANDARUS And she takes upon her to spy a white hair on his chin.

CRESSIDA Alas poor chin, many a wart is richer.

---

104 *a merry Greek* i.e. light of heart and morals 106 *compassed* bay 112 *lifter* thief 125 *addle* rotten, spoiled 131 *rack* torture

PANDARUS But there was such laughing : Queen Hecuba laughed that her eyes ran o'er.

CRESSIDA With millstones. 137

PANDARUS And Cassandra laughed.

CRESSIDA But there was a more temperate fire under the pot of her eyes. Did her eyes run o'er too ?

PANDARUS And Hector laughed.

CRESSIDA At what was all this laughing ?

PANDARUS Marry, at the white hair that Helen spied on Troilus' chin.

CRESSIDA An't had been a green hair, I should have laughed too.

PANDARUS They laughed not so much at the hair as at his pretty answer.

CRESSIDA What was his answer ?

PANDARUS Quoth she, 'Here's but two-and-fifty hairs 150
on your chin, and one of them is white.'

CRESSIDA This is her question.

PANDARUS That's true ; make no question of that. 'Two-and-fifty hairs,' quoth he, 'and one white. That white hair is my father, and all the rest are his sons.' 'Jupiter !' quoth she, 'which of these hairs is Paris, my husband ?' 'The forked one,' quoth he ; 'pluck't out, and give it 157
him.' But there was such laughing, and Helen so blushed, and Paris so chafed, and all the rest so laughed, that it passed.

CRESSIDA So let it now, for it has been a great while going by.

PANDARUS Well, cousin, I told you a thing yesterday ; think on't.

CRESSIDA So I do.

PANDARUS I'll be sworn 'tis true ; he will weep you, an 164
'twere a man born in April. 165

    Sound a retreat.

---

137 *millstones* i.e. obviously not tears 157 *forked* (like a cuckold's horns)
164 *an* as if 165–67 *April . . . May* i.e. April showers bring May flowers

CRESSIDA And I'll spring up in his tears, an 'twere a
nettle against May.

PANDARUS Hark, they are coming from the field. Shall
we stand up here and see them as they pass toward
Ilium ? Good niece, do ; sweet niece, Cressida.

CRESSIDA At your pleasure.

PANDARUS Here, here, here's an excellent place ; here we
173 may see most bravely. I'll tell you them all by their
names as they pass by, but mark Troilus above the rest.

Enter Aeneas [passing across the stage].

CRESSIDA Speak not so loud.

PANDARUS That's Aeneas. Is not that a brave man ? He's
one of the flowers of Troy, I can tell you. But mark
Troilus ; you shall see anon.

Enter Antenor [passing across the stage].

CRESSIDA Who's that ?

PANDARUS That's Antenor. He has a shrewd wit, I can tell
you ; and he's a man good enough : he's one o' th' sound-
182 est judgments in Troy whosoever, and a proper man of
person. When comes Troilus ? I'll show you Troilus
anon. If he see me, you shall see him nod at me.

185 CRESSIDA Will he give you the nod ?

PANDARUS You shall see.

187 CRESSIDA If he do, the rich shall have more.

Enter Hector [passing across the stage].

PANDARUS That's Hector, that, that, look you, that ;
there's a fellow ! Go thy way, Hector ! There's a brave
man, niece. O brave Hector ! Look how he looks ; there's
a countenance ! Is't not a brave man ?

CRESSIDA O, a brave man !

PANDARUS Is 'a not ? It does a man's heart good. Look
you what hacks are on his helmet. Look you yonder, do
you see ? Look you there. There's no jesting ; there's

---

173 *bravely* excellently   182 *proper* good-looking   185 *nod* (quibble on
'noddy,' simpleton)   187 *the rich . . . more* the simple-minded will become
simpler

laying on, take't off who will, as they say. There be 196
hacks!

CRESSIDA Be those with swords?

PANDARUS Swords, anything; he cares not; an the devil
come to him, it's all one. By God's lid, it does one's
heart good.

Enter Paris [passing across the stage].

Yonder comes Paris, yonder comes Paris. Look ye
yonder, niece. Is't not a gallant man too, is't not? Why, 202
this is brave now. Who said he came hurt home to-day?
He's not hurt. Why, this will do Helen's heart good
now, ha! Would I could see Troilus now. You shall see
Troilus anon.

CRESSIDA Who's that?

Enter Helenus [passing across the stage].

PANDARUS That's Helenus. I marvel where Troilus is.
That's Helenus. I think he went not forth to-day.
That's Helenus.

CRESSIDA Can Helenus fight, uncle? 210

PANDARUS Helenus? No. Yes, he'll fight indifferent
well. I marvel where Troilus is. Hark, do you not hear
the people cry 'Troilus'? Helenus is a priest.

CRESSIDA What sneaking fellow comes yonder?

Enter Troilus [passing across the stage].

PANDARUS Where? Yonder? That's Deiphobus. 'Tis
Troilus! There's a man, niece! Hem! Brave Troilus,
the prince of chivalry!

CRESSIDA Peace, for shame, peace!

PANDARUS Mark him, note him. O brave Troilus! Look
well upon him, niece. Look you how his sword is blood-
ied, and his helm more hacked than Hector's; and how
he looks, and how he goes. O admirable youth! he never
saw three-and-twenty. Go thy way, Troilus, go thy

---

196 *laying on* fighting; *take't off who will* i.e. regardless of circumstances
('take off' being a proverbial tag to 'lay on')   202 *gallant* (a general epithet
of praise)   210 *Can Helenus fight* i.e. being a priest

224   way! Had I a sister were a grace, or a daughter a goddess, he should take his choice. O admirable man! Paris?
Paris is dirt to him; and I warrant Helen, to change,
would give an eye to boot.

    [Enter Common Soldiers.]

CRESSIDA Here comes more.

PANDARUS Asses, fools, dolts; chaff and bran, chaff and
bran; porridge after meat. I could live and die in the
eyes of Troilus. Ne'er look, ne'er look. The eagles are
gone; crows and daws, crows and daws. I had rather be
such a man as Troilus than Agamemnon and all Greece.

CRESSIDA There is amongst the Greeks Achilles, a better
man than Troilus.

PANDARUS Achilles? A drayman, a porter, a very camel.

CRESSIDA Well, well.

PANDARUS 'Well, well'? Why, have you any discretion,
have you any eyes, do you know what a man is? Is not
birth, beauty, good shape, discourse, manhood, learn-
ing, gentleness, virtue, youth, liberality, and such like,
the spice and salt that season a man?

243 CRESSIDA Ay, a minced man; and then to be baked with
no date in the pie, for then the man's date is out.

PANDARUS You are such a woman a man knows not at
246   what ward you lie.

CRESSIDA Upon my back, to defend my belly; upon my
wit, to defend my wiles; upon my secrecy, to defend
249   mine honesty; my mask, to defend my beauty; and you,
to defend all these: and at all these wards I lie, at a
thousand watches.

252 PANDARUS Say one of your watches.

CRESSIDA Nay, I'll watch you for that; and that's one of
the chiefest of them too. If I cannot ward what I would
255   not have hit, I can watch you for telling how I took the

---

224 *grace* subordinate and attendant goddess   243 *minced* simpering
246 *ward* posture of defense (fencing term)   249 *honesty* chastity   252
watches i.e. at night   255 *watch you* i.e. make sure that you do not tell (this
passage fully establishes Cressida's moral level)

blow ; unless it swell past hiding, and then it's past
watching.

PANDARUS You are such another !

Enter [Troilus'] Boy.

BOY Sir, my lord would instantly speak with you.

PANDARUS Where ?

BOY At your own house. There he unarms him.

PANDARUS Good boy, tell him I come. *[Exit Boy.]* I doubt
he be hurt. Fare ye well, good niece.

CRESSIDA Adieu, uncle.

PANDARUS I will be with you, niece, by and by.

CRESSIDA To bring, uncle ?   265

PANDARUS Ay, a token from Troilus.

CRESSIDA By the same token, you are a bawd.

[Exit Pandarus.]

Words, vows, gifts, tears, and love's full sacrifice
He offers in another's enterprise ;
But more in Troilus thousandfold I see
Than in the glass of Pandar's praise may be.
Yet hold I off : women are angels, wooing ;   272
Things won are done, joy's soul lies in the doing.
That she beloved knows nought that knows not this :
Men prize the thing ungained more than it is ;   275
That she was never yet, that ever knew
Love got so sweet as when desire did sue.   277
Therefore this maxim out of love I teach :   278
Achievement is command ; ungained, beseech.   279
Then, though my heart's content firm love doth bear,
Nothing of that shall from mine eyes appear.

Exit.

*

265 *bring* get even   272 *wooing* while being wooed   275 *it is* its value
277 *got* i.e. by men   278 *out of love* as taught by love   279 *Achievement
. . . beseech* having achieved love, men command; when trying to gain it,
they beseech

I, iii   *[Sennet.] Enter Agamemnon, Nestor, Ulysses,*
               Diomedes, Menelaus, with others.

AGAMEMNON
    Princes,
    What grief hath set the jaundice on your cheeks?
    The ample proposition that hope makes
    In all designs begun on earth below
    Fails in the promised largeness. Checks and disasters
    Grow in the veins of actions highest reared,
7   As knots, by the conflux of meeting sap,
    Infects the sound pine and diverts his grain
9   Tortive and errant from his course of growth.
    Nor, princes, is it matter new to us
11 That we come short of our suppose so far
    That after seven years' siege yet Troy walls stand;
    Sith every action that hath gone before,
    Whereof we have record, trial did draw
15 Bias and thwart, not answering the aim
    And that unbodied figure of the thought
    That gave't surmisèd shape. Why then, you princes,
    Do you with cheeks abashed behold our works
    And call them shames, which are indeed nought else
    But the protractive trials of great Jove
    To find persistive constancy in men?
    The fineness of which metal is not found
    In Fortune's love; for then, the bold and coward,
24 The wise and fool, the artist and unread,
25 The hard and soft, seem all affined and kin.
    But, in the wind and tempest of her frown,
    Distinction, with a broad and powerful fan,
    Puffing at all, winnows the light away;
    And what hath mass or matter by itself

I, iii The Grecian camp **s.d.** *Sennet* a conventional sequence of trumpet notes to indicate a procession **7** *conflux* flowing together **9** *Tortive and errant* distorted and wandering **11** *suppose* expectation **15** *Bias and thwart* to one side and crosswise **24** *artist* scholar in the liberal arts **25** *affined* in affinity

Lies rich in virtue and unmingled.   30

NESTOR

With duc observance of thy godlike seat,
Great Agamemnon, Nestor shall apply
Thy latest words. In the reproof of chance
Lies the true proof of men. The sea being smooth,
How many shallow bauble boats dare sail
Upon her patient breast, making their way
With those of nobler bulk ?
But let the ruffian Boreas once enrage   38
The gentle Thetis, and anon behold   39
The strong-ribbed bark through liquid mountains cut,
Bounding between the two moist elements
Like Perseus' horse, where's then the saucy boat,   42
Whose weak untimbered sides but even now
Co-rivalled greatness ? Either to harbor fled,
Or made a toast for Neptune. Even so   45
Doth valor's show and valor's worth divide
In storms of fortune. For in her ray and brightness
The herd hath more annoyance by the breese   48
Than by the tiger ; but when the splitting wind
Makes flexible the knees of knotted oaks,
And flies fled under shade, why then the thing of courage,
As roused with rage, with rage doth sympathize,
And with an accent tuned in self-same key
Returns to chiding fortune.   54

ULYSSES   Agamemnon,
Thou great commander, nerves and bone of Greece,   55
Heart of our numbers, soul and only spirit,
In whom the tempers and the minds of all
Should be shut up, hear what Ulysses speaks.   58
Besides th' applause and approbation

---

30 *unmingled* unalloyed   38 *Boreas* north wind   39 *Thetis* a Nereid or sea-
maiden, mother of Achilles, here personifying the sea   42 *Perseus' horse*
the winged horse Pegasus, which sprang from Medusa's blood after
Perseus beheaded her   45 *toast* a piece of toast put into liquor   48 *breese*
gadfly   54 *Returns* answers back   55 *nerves* sinews   58 *shut up* gathered in

The which, *[to Agamemnon]* most mighty for thy place
   and sway,
     [To Nestor]
And thou most reverend for thy stretched-out life,
I give to both your speeches, which were such
As Agamemnon and the hand of Greece
Should hold up high in brass; and such again
65   As venerable Nestor, hatched in silver,
Should with a bond of air, strong as the axle-tree
On which heaven rides, knit all the Greekish ears
To his experienced tongue; yet let it please both,
Thou great, and wise, to hear Ulysses speak.

[AGAMEMNON
Speak, Prince of Ithaca; and be't of less expect
That matter needless, of importless burden,
Divide thy lips than we are confident,
73   When rank Thersites opes his mastic jaws,
We shall hear music, wit, and oracle.]

ULYSSES
Troy, yet upon his basis, had been down,
And the great Hector's sword had lacked a master,
But for these instances.
78   The specialty of rule hath been neglected;
And look, how many Grecian tents do stand
Hollow upon this plain, so many hollow factions.
When that the general is not like the hive
To whom the foragers shall all repair,
83   What honey is expected? Degree being vizarded,
Th' unworthiest shows as fairly in the mask.
The heavens themselves, the planets, and this centre
Observe degree, priority, and place,
87   Insisture, course, proportion, season, form,
Office, and custom, in all line of order.

---

65 *hatched in silver* with silver lines in his hair   73 *mastic* abusive (from
Greek 'scourge')   78 *specialty of rule* particular rights of supreme authority
83 *Degree being vizarded* the hierarchy of authority being hidden **87**
Insisture regularity of position

And therefore is the glorious planet Sol   89
In noble eminence enthroned and sphered
Amidst the other ; whose med'cinable eye   91
Corrects the influence of evil planets,   92
And posts, like the commandment of a king,
Sans check to good and bad. But when the planets
In evil mixture to disorder wander,
What plagues, and what portents, what mutiny,
What raging of the sea, shaking of earth,
Commotion in the winds, frights, changes, horrors,
Divert and crack, rend and deracinate   99
The unity and married calm of states
Quite from their fixure ? O, when degree is shaked,
Which is the ladder of all high designs,
The enterprise is sick. How could communities,
Degrees in schools, and brotherhoods in cities,
Peaceful commerce from dividable shores,
The primogenity and due of birth,   106
Prerogative of age, crowns, sceptres, laurels,
But by degree, stand in authentic place ?
Take but degree away, untune that string,
And hark what discord follows. Each thing meets
In mere oppugnancy. The bounded waters   111
Should lift their bosoms higher than the shores
And make a sop of all this solid globe ;   113
Strength should be lord of imbecility,   114
And the rude son should strike his father dead ;
Force should be right, or rather right and wrong,
Between whose endless jar justice resides,   117
Should lose their names, and so should justice too ;
Then everything include itself in power,   119
Power into will, will into appetite.

89 *Sol* sun **91** *other* others **92** *influence* astrological effect **99** *de-racinate* uproot **106** *primogenity* right of the eldest son to succeed **111** *mere oppugnancy* total strife **113** *sop* pulp **114** *imbecility* weakness **117** *jar* collision **119** *include itself in* should confine itself within, i.e. convert itself into

And appetite, an universal wolf,
So doubly seconded with will and power,
Must make perforce an universal prey
And last eat up himself. Great Agamemnon,
125   This chaos, when degree is suffocate,
Follows the choking.
127   And this neglection of degree it is
128   That by a pace goes backward with a purpose
It hath to climb. The general's disdained
By him one step below, he by the next,
That next by him beneath; so every step,
132   Exampled by the first pace that is sick
Of his superior, grows to an envious fever
Of pale and bloodless emulation:
And 'tis this fever that keeps Troy on foot,
Not her own sinews. To end a tale of length,
Troy in our weakness stands, not in her strength.

NESTOR
Most wisely hath Ulysses here discovered
The fever whereof all our power is sick.

AGAMEMNON
The nature of the sickness found, Ulysses,
What is the remedy?

ULYSSES
The great Achilles, whom opinion crowns
The sinew and the forehand of our host,
Having his ear full of his airy fame,
145   Grows dainty of his worth, and in his tent
Lies mocking our designs. With him Patroclus
Upon a lazy bed the livelong day
Breaks scurril jests,
And with ridiculous and silly action

---

125 *chaos* raw matter without form or order   127 *neglection* neglect
128–29 *by a pace . . . climb* step by step goes backward when it is trying to
climb   132–33 *Exampled . . . superior* taking its example from the first
step that someone takes against his superior   145 *dainty of* particular about

(Which, slanderer, he imitation calls)
He pageants us. Sometime, great Agamemnon, 151
Thy topless deputation he puts on 152
And, like a strutting player, whose conceit
Lies in his hamstring, and doth think it rich 154
To hear the wooden dialogue and sound
'Twixt his stretched footing and the scaffoldage, 156
Such to-be-pitied and o'er-wrested seeming
He acts thy greatness in; and when he speaks,
'Tis like a chime a-mending, with terms unsquared, 159
Which, from the tongue of roaring Typhon dropped, 160
Would seem hyperboles. At this fusty stuff
The large Achilles, on his pressed bed lolling,
From his deep chest laughs out a loud applause,
Cries, 'Excellent! 'tis Agamemnon right.
Now play me Nestor; hem, and stroke thy beard,
As he being drest to some oration.'
That's done, as near as the extremest ends
Of parallels, as like as Vulcan and his wife, 168
Yet god Achilles still cries, 'Excellent!
'Tis Nestor right. Now play him me, Patroclus,
Arming to answer in a night alarm.'
And then, forsooth, the faint defects of age
Must be the scene of mirth; to cough and spit,
And with a palsy fumbling on his gorget, 174
Shake in and out the rivet; and at this sport
Sir Valor dies; cries, 'O! enough, Patroclus,
Or give me ribs of steel; I shall split all
In pleasure of my spleen.' And in this fashion 178
All our abilities, gifts, natures, shapes,

---

151 *pageants* acts or mimics **152** *topless deputation* supreme authority
154 *hamstring* tendon at the back of the knee **156** *scaffoldage* stage **159**
unsquared unsuited **160** *Typhon* a monster with serpents' heads and a
tremendous voice, overwhelmed by Zeus with thunderbolts **168** *Vulcan
and his wife* (the beautiful Venus cuckolded Vulcan, who was lame and
sooty, with Mars) **174** *gorget* throat armor **178** *spleen* (regarded as the
seat of the emotions of anger and hilarity)

180   Severals and generals of grace exact,
       Achievements, plots, orders, preventions,
       Excitements to the field or speech for truce,
       Success or loss, what is or is not, serves
184   As stuff for these two to make paradoxes.

NESTOR
       And in the imitation of these twain,
       Who, as Ulysses says, opinion crowns
       With an imperial voice, many are infect.
       Ajax is grown self-willed, and bears his head
189   In such a rein, in full as proud a place
       As broad Achilles ; keeps his tent like him ;
       Makes factious feasts ; rails on our state of war,
       Bold as an oracle, and sets Thersites,
193   A slave whose gall coins slanders like a mint,
       To match us in comparisons with dirt,
       To weaken and discredit our exposure,
196   How rank soever rounded in with danger.

ULYSSES
       They tax our policy and call it cowardice,
       Count wisdom as no member of the war,
199   Forestall prescience, and esteem no act
       But that of hand. The still and mental parts
       That do contrive how many hands shall strike
       When fitness calls them on, and know by measure
       Of their observant toil the enemies' weight –
       Why, this hath not a finger's dignity.
205   They call this bed-work, mapp'ry, closet-war ;
       So that the ram that batters down the wall,
207   For the great swinge and rudeness of his poise,
       They place before his hand that made the engine,
       Or those that with the fineness of their souls
       By reason guide his execution.

---

180 *Severals and generals* individual and common excellences 184
paradoxes absurdities   189 *In such a rein* so high   193 *gall* source of bile, a
humor conducive to rancor   196 *rank* abundantly   199 *Forestall prescience*
discount foresight   205 *mapp'ry* map-making   207 *swinge* impetus

NESTOR

    Let this be granted, and Achilles' horse   211

    Makes many Thetis' sons.   212

          Tucket.

AGAMEMNON

    What trumpet? Look, Menelaus.

MENELAUS

    From Troy.

          Enter Aeneas.

AGAMEMNON

    What would you 'fore our tent?

AENEAS

    Is this great Agamemnon's tent, I pray you?

AGAMEMNON

    Even this.

AENEAS

    May one that is a herald and a prince

    Do a fair message to his kingly eyes?   219

AGAMEMNON

    With surety stronger than Achilles' arm

    'Fore all the Greekish heads, which with one voice

    Call Agamemnon head and general.

AENEAS

    Fair leave and large security. How may

    A stranger to those most imperial looks

    Know them from eyes of other mortals?

AGAMEMNON   How?

AENEAS

    Ay.

    I ask, that I might waken reverence,

    And bid the cheek be ready with a blush

    Modest as morning when she coldly eyes

    The youthful Phoebus,   230

    Which is that god in office, guiding men?

---

211 *horse* (either literally or collectively for his horsemen, i.e. Myrmidons)
212 s.d. *Tucket* preparatory signal on a trumpet   219 *to . . . eyes* i.e. in his presence   230 *Phoebus* Apollo, the sun god

Which is the high and mighty Agamemnon?

AGAMEMNON

This Troyan scorns us, or the men of Troy
Are ceremonious courtiers.

AENEAS

Courtiers as free, as debonair, unarmed,
As bending angels; that's their fame in peace.
But when they would seem soldiers, they have galls,
238   Good arms, strong joints, true swords; and, Jove's
accord,
Nothing so full of heart. But peace, Aeneas;
Peace, Troyan; lay thy finger on thy lips.
The worthiness of praise distains his worth,
If that the praised himself bring the praise forth.
But what the repining enemy commends,
That breath fame blows; that praise, sole pure, trans-
cends.

AGAMEMNON

Sir, you of Troy, call you yourself Aeneas?

AENEAS

Ay, Greek, that is my name.

AGAMEMNON

What's your affair, I pray you?

AENEAS

Sir, pardon; 'tis for Agamemnon's ears.

AGAMEMNON

He hears nought privately that comes from Troy.

AENEAS

Nor I from Troy come not to whisper him:
I bring a trumpet to awake his ear,
252   To set his seat on the attentive bent,
And then to speak.

AGAMEMNON   Speak frankly as the wind;
It is not Agamemnon's sleeping hour.
That thou shalt know, Troyan, he is awake,

238 *Jove's accord* if Jove favor them, i.e. with God on their side   252 *To
set . . . bent* i.e. to make him sit up and take notice

He tells thee so himself.

AENEAS   Trumpet, blow loud,
Send thy brass voice through all these lazy tents;
And every Greek of mettle, let him know,
What Troy means fairly shall be spoke aloud.
        Sound trumpet.
We have, great Agamemnon, here in Troy
A prince called Hector – Priam is his father –
Who in this dull and long-continued truce
Is rusty grown. He bade me take a trumpet,
And to this purpose speak: Kings, princes, lords,
If there be one among the fair'st of Greece
That holds his honor higher than his ease,
That seeks his praise more than he fears his peril,
That knows his valor and knows not his fear,
That loves his mistress more than in confession   269
With truant vows to her own lips he loves,
And dare avow her beauty and her worth
In other arms than hers – to him this challenge.
Hector, in view of Troyans and of Greeks,
Shall make it good, or do his best to do it,
He hath a lady wiser, fairer, truer,
Than ever Greek did compass in his arms;
And will to-morrow with his trumpet call,
Midway between your tents and walls of Troy,
To rouse a Grecian that is true in love.
If any come, Hector shall honor him;
If none, he'll say in Troy when he retires,
The Grecian dames are sunburnt and not worth   282
The splinter of a lance. Even so much.

AGAMEMNON
This shall be told our lovers, Lord Aeneas;
If none of them have soul in such a kind,
We left them all at home. But we are soldiers;
And may that soldier a mere recreant prove,

269–70 *more . . . loves* more than enough to swear false vows that he loves
her   282 *sunburnt* dark, i.e. ugly

That means not, hath not, or is not in love!
If then one is, or hath, or means to be,
That one meets Hector; if none else, I am he.

NESTOR

Tell him of Nestor, one that was a man
When Hector's grandsire sucked. He is old now,
But if there be not in our Grecian host
A noble man that hath one spark of fire
To answer for his love, tell him from me,
296 I'll hide my silver beard in a gold beaver,
297 And in my vantbrace put this withered brawn,
And, meeting him, will tell him that my lady
Was fairer than his grandam, and as chaste
As may be in the world. His youth in flood,
I'll prove this troth with my three drops of blood.

AENEAS

Now heavens forfend such scarcity of youth!

ULYSSES

Amen.

AGAMEMNON

For Lord Aeneas, let me touch your hand;
To our pavilion shall I lead you first.
Achilles shall have word of this intent;
So shall each lord of Greece, from tent to tent.
Yourself shall feast with us before you go,
And find the welcome of a noble foe.

[Exeunt. Manent Ulysses and Nestor.]

ULYSSES

Nestor.

NESTOR

What says Ulysses?

ULYSSES

312 I have a young conception in my brain;
Be you my time to bring it to some shape.

296 *beaver* face-guard of a helmet   297 *vantbrace* armor for the forearm
312–13 *I have . . . shape* I have conceived a bright idea; listen while I
develop it

NESTOR
What is't?
ULYSSES
[This 'tis :]
Blunt wedges rive hard knots ; the seeded pride
That hath to this maturity blown up
In rank Achilles, must or now be cropped
Or, shedding, breed a nursery of like evil   319
To overbulk us all.
NESTOR   Well, and how ?
ULYSSES
This challenge that the gallant Hector sends,
However it is spread in general name,
Relates in purpose only to Achilles.
NESTOR
True, the purpose is perspicuous as substance
Whose grossness little characters sum up ;   325
And, in the publication, make no strain   326
But that Achilles, were his brain as barren
As banks of Libya – though, Apollo knows,
'Tis dry enough – will with great speed of judgment,
Ay with celerity, find Hector's purpose
Pointing on him.
ULYSSES
And wake him to the answer, think you ?
NESTOR
Why, 'tis most meet. Who may you else oppose
That can from Hector bring his honor off,
If not Achilles ? Though 't be a sportful combat,
Yet in this trial much opinion dwells ;   336
For here the Troyans taste our dear'st repute
With their fin'st palate ; and trust to me, Ulysses,
Our imputation shall be oddly poised   339

319 *shedding* i.e. scattering its seed   325 *grossness . . . up* great size little
figures describe   326 *make no strain* have no difficulty in understanding
336 *opinion* reputation   339 *imputation* reputation; *oddly poised* unequally
balanced

340 In this vild action. For the success,
341 Although particular, shall give a scantling
342 Of good or bad unto the general;
343 And in such indexes, although small pricks
To their subsequent volumes, there is seen
The baby figure of the giant mass
Of things to come at large. It is supposed
He that meets Hector issues from our choice;
And choice, being mutual act of all our souls,
349 Makes merit her election, and doth boil,
As 'twere from forth us all, a man distilled
Out of our virtues; who miscarrying,
What heart receives from hence a conquering part,
To steel a strong opinion to themselves!
354 [Which entertained, limbs are his instruments,
In no less working than are swords and bows
Directive by the limbs.]

ULYSSES
Give pardon to my speech: therefore 'tis meet
Achilles meet not Hector. Let us, like merchants,
First show foul wares, and think perchance they'll sell;
If not, the lustre of the better shall exceed
By showing the worse first. Do not consent
That ever Hector and Achilles meet;
For both our honor and our shame in this
364 Are dogged with two strange followers.

NESTOR
I see them not with my old eyes. What are they?

ULYSSES
What glory our Achilles shares from Hector,
Were he not proud, we all should share with him.
But he already is too insolent,

340 *vild* trivial   341 *scantling* sample   342 *general* entire army   343–44 *small . . . volumes* small marks in comparison to the volumes that follow 349 *election* basis of choice   354 *his* its, i.e. the strong opinion's   364 *followers* consequences

And we were better parch in Afric sun
Than in the pride and salt scorn of his eyes,   370
Should he 'scape Hector fair. If he were foiled,
Why then we did our main opinion crush   372
In taint of our best man. No, make a lott'ry ;
And by device let blockish Ajax draw
The sort to fight with Hector ; among ourselves
Give him allowance for the better man,
For that will physic the great Myrmidon   377
Who broils in loud applause, and make him fall   378
His crest that prouder than blue Iris bends.   379
If the dull brainless Ajax comes safe off,
We'll dress him up in voices ; if he fail,
Yet go we under our opinion still
That we have better men. But, hit or miss,
Our project's life this shape of sense assumes :
Ajax employed plucks down Achilles' plumes.

NESTOR

Now, Ulysses, I begin to relish thy advice,
And I will give a taste thereof forthwith
To Agamemnon. Go we to him straight.
Two curs shall tame each other ; pride alone
Must tarre the mastiffs on, as 'twere a bone.   *Exeunt.* 390

*

Enter Ajax and Thersites.   II, i

AJAX Thersites!
THERSITES Agamemnon, how if he had biles – full, all   2
over, generally ?
AJAX Thersites!

---

370 *salt* bitter   372 *our main opinion* the chief source of our reputation
377 *Myrmidon* Achilles, son of Peleus, whose subjects, created by Zeus out
of ants (myrmekes), were called Myrmidons   378 *broils* i.e. suns himself
379 *Iris* the rainbow   390 *tarre* incite to fight
II, i The Grecian camp   2 *biles* boils

5 THERSITES And those biles did run? – say so. Did not
6 the general run then? Were not that a botchy core?

AJAX Dog!

THERSITES Then would come some matter from him. I
see none now.

AJAX Thou bitch-wolf's son, canst thou not hear? Feel
then.

[Strikes him.]

11 THERSITES The plague of Greece upon thee, thou mongrel beef-witted lord!

13 AJAX Speak then, thou vinewed'st leaven, speak. I will
beat thee into handsomeness.

THERSITES I shall sooner rail thee into wit and holiness;
16 but I think thy horse will sooner con an oration than
17 thou learn a prayer without book. Thou canst strike,
18 canst thou? A red murrain o' thy jade's tricks!

19 AJAX Toadstool, learn me the proclamation.

THERSITES Dost thou think I have no sense, thou strikest
me thus?

AJAX The proclamation!

THERSITES Thou art proclaimed fool, I think.

24 AJAX Do not, porpentine, do not; my fingers itch.

THERSITES I would thou didst itch from head to foot; an
I had the scratching of thee, I would make thee the
loathsomest scab in Greece. When thou art forth in the
28 incursions, thou strikest as slow as another.

AJAX I say, the proclamation!

THERSITES Thou grumblest and railest every hour on
Achilles, and thou art as full of envy at his greatness as
32 Cerberus is at Proserpina's beauty, ay that thou bark'st
at him.

---

5 *biles* boils   6 *botchy core* inflamed boil   11 *plague of Greece* (probably an
allusion to a plague sent by Apollo upon the Greek army)   13 *vinewed'st*
most mouldy   16 *con* learn by heart   17 *without book* by heart   18 *murrain*
plague; *jade's* broken-down horse's   19 *learn me* find out for me   24 *porpentine* porcupine   28 *incursions* attacks upon the Trojans   32 *Cerberus*
watchdog of Hades; *Proserpina* a beautiful goddess carried off by Hades or
Pluto for his bride

AJAX Mistress Thersites!

THERSITES Thou shouldst strike him.

AJAX Cobloaf!   35

THERSITES He would pun thee into shivers with his fist,   36
as a sailor breaks a biscuit.

AJAX You whoreson cur!
        [Beating him.]

THERSITES Do, do.

AJAX Thou stool for a witch!

THERSITES Ay, do, do, thou sodden-witted lord! thou
hast no more brain than I have in mine elbows; an asinico   42
may tutor thee. Thou scurvy-valiant ass, thou art here
but to thrash Troyans, and thou art bought and sold   44
among those of any wit like a barbarian slave. If thou use
to beat me, I will begin at thy heel, and tell what thou
art by inches, thou thing of no bowels, thou!   47

AJAX You dog!

THERSITES You scurvy lord!

AJAX You cur!
        [Beating him.]

THERSITES Mars his idiot! Do, rudeness; do, camel; do,   51
do.

        [Enter Achilles and Patroclus.]

ACHILLES Why, how now, Ajax, wherefore do ye thus?
How now, Thersites, what's the matter, man?

THERSITES You see him there, do you?

ACHILLES Ay, what's the matter?

THERSITES Nay, look upon him.

ACHILLES So I do. What's the matter?

THERSITES Nay, but regard him well.

ACHILLES 'Well' – why so I do.

THERSITES But yet you look not well upon him; for,
whosomever you take him to be, he is Ajax.   61

ACHILLES I know that, fool.

---

35 *Cobloaf* a crusty uneven loaf of bread   36 *pun* pound   42 *asinico* little
ass   44 *bought and sold* i.e. made sport of   47 *bowels* i.e. bowels of mercy
51 *Mars his* Mars's   61 *whosomever* whomsoever

63 THERSITES Ay, but that fool knows not himself.

AJAX Therefore I beat thee.

THERSITES Lo, lo, lo, lo, what modicums of wit he
66 utters! His evasions have ears thus long. I have bobbed
his brain more than he has beat my bones. I will buy
68 nine sparrows for a penny, and his pia mater is not
worth the ninth part of a sparrow. This lord, Achilles,
Ajax, who wears his wit in his belly and his guts in his
head, I'll tell you what I say of him.

ACHILLES What?

THERSITES I say, this Ajax –
[Ajax offers to strike him.]

ACHILLES Nay, good Ajax.

THERSITES Has not so much wit –
[Ajax again offers to strike him.]

ACHILLES Nay, I must hold you.

THERSITES As will stop the eye of Helen's needle, for
whom he comes to fight.

ACHILLES Peace, fool!

THERSITES I would have peace and quietness, but the
fool will not – he there, that he. Look you there.

AJAX O thou damned cur, I shall –

83 ACHILLES Will you set your wit to a fool's?

THERSITES No, I warrant you; the fool's will shame it.

PATROCLUS Good words, Thersites.

ACHILLES What's the quarrel?

AJAX I bade the vile owl go learn me the tenor of the
proclamation, and he rails upon me.

THERSITES I serve thee not.

AJAX Well, go to, go to.

THERSITES I serve here voluntary.

ACHILLES Your last service was sufferance, 'twas not
voluntary; no man is beaten voluntary. Ajax was here

---

63 *that fool* (Thersites pretends that Achilles said, 'I know that fool') 66
have ears thus long i.e. are those of an ass; *bobbed* thumped 68 *pia mater*
(here the brain itself) 83 *set . . . fool's* match wits with a fool

58

the voluntary, and you as under an impress. 94

THERSITES E'en so. A great deal of your wit, too, lies in your sinews, or else there be liars. Hector shall have a great catch if he knock out either of your brains. 'A were as good crack a fusty nut with no kernel.

ACHILLES What, with me too, Thersites?

THERSITES There's Ulysses and old Nestor, whose wit was mouldy ere your grandsires had nails on their toes, yoke you like draught-oxen and make you plough up the wars.

ACHILLES What, what?

THERSITES Yes, good sooth. To, Achilles; to, Ajax; to – 104

AJAX I shall cut out your tongue.

THERSITES 'Tis no matter; I shall speak as much as thou afterwards.

PATROCLUS No more words, Thersites; peace!

THERSITES I will hold my peace when Achilles' brach 109 bids me, shall I?

ACHILLES There's for you, Patroclus.

THERSITES I will see you hanged, like clotpoles, ere I 112 come any more to your tents. I will keep where there is wit stirring and leave the faction of fools. *Exit.*

PATROCLUS A good riddance.

ACHILLES

Marry, this, sir, is proclaimed through all our host: 116

That Hector, by the fifth hour of the sun, 117

Will, with a trumpet, 'twixt our tents and Troy

To-morrow morning call some knight to arms

That hath a stomach, and such a one that dare

Maintain – I know not what; 'tis trash. Farewell.

AJAX

Farewell? Who shall answer him?

---

94 *impress* (pun on impressment into military service) 104 *To . . . Ajax* (Achilles and Ajax are compared to horses being urged on by a driver) 109 *brach* bitch 112 *clotpoles* blockheads 116 *Marry* why, indeed (originally an oath by the Virgin Mary) 117 *fifth hour* i.e. 11 a.m.

ACHILLES
I know not. 'Tis put to lott'ry. Otherwise,
He knew his man.

AJAX
O, meaning you ? I will go learn more of it.   *[Exeunt.]*

*

II, ii   *Enter Priam, Hector, Troilus, Paris, and Helenus.*

PRIAM
After so many hours, lives, speeches spent,
Thus once again says Nestor from the Greeks :
'Deliver Helen, and all damage else,
As honor, loss of time, travail, expense,
Wounds, friends, and what else dear that is consumed
6   In hot digestion of this cormorant war,
Shall be struck off.' Hector, what say you to't ?

HECTOR
Though no man lesser fears the Greeks than I,
9   As far as toucheth my particular,
Yet, dread Priam,
There is no lady of more softer bowels,
More spongy to suck in the sense of fear,
More ready to cry out, 'Who knows what follows ?'
14   Than Hector is. The wound of peace is surety,
Surety secure ; but modest doubt is called
16   The beacon of the wise, the tent that searches
To th' bottom of the worst. Let Helen go.
Since the first sword was drawn about this question,
19   Every tithe soul, 'mongst many thousand dismes,
Hath been as dear as Helen ; I mean, of ours.
If we have lost so many tenths of ours
To guard a thing not ours nor worth to us,

II, ii The palace of Priam   6 *cormorant* ravenous   9 *my particular* me
personally   14 *The . . . surety* our sense of security imperils peace   16
tent lint for probing wounds   19 *Every . . . dismes* every soul taken by
war as its tenth among many thousand such tenths

Had it our name, the value of one ten,
What merit 's in that reason which denies
The yielding of her up?

TROILUS   Fie, fie, my brother!
Weigh you the worth and honor of a king
So great as our dread father in a scale
Of common ounces? Will you with counters sum   28
The past proportion of his infinite,   29
And buckle in a waist most fathomless
With spans and inches so diminutive   31
As fears and reasons? Fie, for godly shame!

HELENUS
No marvel, though you bite so sharp at reasons,
You are so empty of them. Should not our father
Bear the great sway of his affairs with reason,
Because your speech hath none that tell him so?

TROILUS
You are for dreams and slumbers, brother priest;
You fur your gloves with reason. Here are your reasons: 38
You know an enemy intends you harm;
You know a sword employed is perilous,
And reason flies the object of all harm.
Who marvels then, when Helenus beholds
A Grecian and his sword, if he do set
The very wings of reason to his heels
And fly like chidden Mercury from Jove,
Or like a star disorbed? Nay, if we talk of reason,   46
Let's shut our gates and sleep. Manhood and honor
Should have hare-hearts, would they but fat their
    thoughts
With this crammed reason. Reason and respect
Make livers pale and lustihood deject.   50

---

28 *counters* worthless tokens used for counting   **29** *The . . . infinite* his
infinite greatness past comparing by measurement   **31** *spans* measures of
nine inches   **38** *fur . . . reason* use reason in your speech as fur is used to
ornament gloves or to give them a soft, warm lining   **46** *disorbed* thrown
from its sphere   **50** *livers* (regarded as seats of the passions)

HECTOR
   Brother, she is not worth what she doth cost
   The keeping.
TROILUS   What's aught but as 'tis valued?
HECTOR
53   But value dwells not in particular will;
54   It holds his estimate and dignity
   As well wherein 'tis precious of itself
56   As in the prizer. 'Tis mad idolatry
   To make the service greater than the god;
58   And the will dotes that is attributive
59   To what infectiously itself affects,
   Without some image of th' affected merit.
TROILUS
   I take to-day a wife, and my election
   Is led on in the conduct of my will –
   My will enkindled by mine eyes and ears,
64   Two traded pilots 'twixt the dangerous shores
   Of will and judgment. How may I avoid,
   Although my will distaste what it elected,
   The wife I chose? There can be no evasion
68   To blench from this and to stand firm by honor.
   We turn not back the silks upon the merchant
   When we have soiled them, nor the remainder viands
71   We do not throw in unrespective sieve
   Because we now are full. It was thought meet
   Paris should do some vengeance on the Greeks.
   Your breath with full consent bellied his sails;
   The seas and winds, old wranglers, took a truce
   And did him service; he touched the ports desired,
77   And for an old aunt whom the Greeks held captive

---

53 *particular will* the individual's inclination   **54** *dignity* worth   **56** *prizer* appraiser   **58** *attributive* i.e. subservient as is one who pays tribute   **59–60** *To what . . . merit* to what it inclines toward, as if diseased, without some idea of the value it is seeking   **64** *traded* experienced   **68** *blench* shrink   **71** *unrespective sieve* receptacle which does not care what is put into it   **77** *aunt* Hesione, Priam's sister and mother of Ajax

He brought a Grecian queen, whose youth and freshness
Wrinkles Apollo's and makes stale the morning.
Why keep we her? The Grecians keep our aunt.
Is she worth keeping? Why, she is a pearl
Whose price hath launched above a thousand ships   82
And turned crowned kings to merchants.
If you'll avouch 'twas wisdom Paris went –
As you must needs, for you all cried, 'Go, go' –
If you'll confess he brought home worthy prize –
As you must needs, for you all clapped your hands,
And cried, 'Inestimable!' – why do you now
The issue of your proper wisdoms rate,   89
And do a deed that never Fortune did,
Beggar the estimation which you prized   91
Richer than sea and land? O theft most base,
That we have stol'n what we do fear to keep!
But thieves unworthy of a thing so stol'n,
That in their country did them that disgrace   95
We fear to warrant in our native place.   96

CASSANDRA *[within]*
   Cry, Troyans, cry!   97
PRIAM   What noise? what shriek is this?
TROILUS
   'Tis our mad sister. I do know her voice.
CASSANDRA *[within]* Cry, Troyans!
HECTOR   It is Cassandra.
        Enter Cassandra raving [with her hair about her ears].
CASSANDRA
   Cry, Troyans, cry! Lend me ten thousand eyes,
   And I will fill them with prophetic tears.
HECTOR
   Peace, sister, peace!

---

82 *Whose . . . ships* (cf. Marlowe, 'Was this the face that launched a
thousand ships?') 89 *your . . . rate* your own wisdom condemn 91
estimation thing esteemed 95 *disgrace* i.e. the rape of Helen 96 *warrant*
justify by defense 97 *Cassandra* (when she resisted the love of Apollo,
he nullified his former gift of prophecy by causing her never to be believed)

CASSANDRA
    Virgins and boys, mid-age and wrinkled elders,
    Soft infancy, that nothing canst but cry,
    Add to my clamors! Let us pay betimes
107   A moiety of that mass of moan to come.
    Cry, Troyans, cry! Practise your eyes with tears!
    Troy must not be, nor goodly Ilion stand;
110   Our firebrand brother, Paris, burns us all.
    Cry, Troyans, cry! A Helen and a woe!
    Cry, cry! Troy burns, or else let Helen go.   *Exit.*

HECTOR
    Now, youthful Troilus, do not these high strains
    Of divination in our sister work
    Some touches of remorse? Or is your blood
    So madly hot that no discourse of reason,
    Nor fear of bad success in a bad cause,
    Can qualify the same?

TROILUS   Why, brother Hector,
    We may not think the justness of each act
120   Such and no other than event doth form it,
    Nor once deject the courage of our minds
122   Because Cassandra's mad. Her brainsick raptures
123   Cannot distaste the goodness of a quarrel
    Which hath our several honors all engaged
    To make it gracious. For my private part,
    I am no more touched than all Priam's sons;
    And Jove forbid there should be done amongst us
128   Such things as might offend the weakest spleen
    To fight for and maintain.

PARIS
130   Else might the world convince of levity
    As well my undertakings as your counsels;
    But I attest the gods, your full consent

---

107 *moiety* part   110 *firebrand* (his mother dreamed that she was delivered of a firebrand when Paris was born)   120 *event* outcome   122 *raptures* prophetic seizures   123 *distaste* make distasteful   128 *spleen* temper   130 *convince* convict

Gave wings to my propension and cut off   133
All fears attending on so dire a project.
For what, alas, can these my single arms ?
What propugnation is in one man's valor   136
To stand the push and enmity of those
This quarrel would excite ? Yet, I protest,
Were I alone to pass the difficulties,   139
And had as ample power as I have will,
Paris should ne'er retract what he hath done
Nor faint in the pursuit.

PRIAM   Paris, you speak
Like one besotted on your sweet delights.
You have the honey still, but these the gall ;
So to be valiant is no praise at all.

PARIS
Sir, I propose not merely to myself
The pleasures such a beauty brings with it ;
But I would have the soil of her fair rape   148
Wiped off in honorable keeping her.
What treason were it to the ransacked queen,   150
Disgrace to your great worths, and shame to me,
Now to deliver her possession up
On terms of base compulsion ! Can it be
That so degenerate a strain as this
Should once set footing in your generous bosoms ?   155
There's not the meanest spirit on our party
Without a heart to dare or sword to draw
When Helen is defended, nor none so noble
Whose life were ill bestowed or death unfamed
Where Helen is the subject. Then, I say,
Well may we fight for her, whom we know well
The world's large spaces cannot parallel.

HECTOR
Paris and Troilus, you have both said well ;

133 *propension* inclination   136 *propugnation* defense   139 *pass* undergo
148 *rape* carrying off   150 *ransacked* carried off   155 *generous* of noble
birth, and therefore of noble nature

And on the cause and question now in hand
165 Have glozed, but superficially ; not much
Unlike young men, whom Aristotle thought
167 Unfit to hear moral philosophy.
The reasons you allege do more conduce
To the hot passion of distemp'red blood
Than to make up a free determination
'Twixt right and wrong, for pleasure and revenge
172 Have ears more deaf than adders to the voice
Of any true decision. Nature craves
All dues be rend'red to their owners. Now,
What nearer debt in all humanity
Than wife is to the husband ? If this law
177 Of nature be corrupted through affection,
178 And that great minds, of partial indulgence
179 To their benumbèd wills, resist the same,
There is a law in each well-ordered nation
To curb those raging appetites that are
Most disobedient and refractory.
If Helen, then, be wife to Sparta's king,
As it is known she is, these moral laws
Of nature and of nations speak aloud
To have her back returned. Thus to persist
187 In doing wrong extenuates not wrong,
But makes it much more heavy. Hector's opinion
Is this in way of truth ; yet ne'ertheless,
190 My spritely brethren, I propend to you
In resolution to keep Helen still ;
For 'tis a cause that hath no mean dependence
Upon our joint and several dignities.

TROILUS
Why, there you touched the life of our design.

165 *glozed* commented, glossed   167 *moral* (Aristotle wrote 'political,' but
Shakespeare's 'moral' is paralleled in contemporary translations of the
passage)   172 *more deaf than adders* (cf. Psalms lviii, 4–5)   177 *affection*
movement of appetite   178 *partial* favoring   179 *benumbèd* hypnotized
by appetite and insensitive to reason   187 *extenuates* lessens   190 *spritely*
spirited; *propend* incline

Were it not glory that we more affected
Than the performance of our heaving spleens,   196
I would not wish a drop of Troyan blood
Spent more in her defense. But, worthy Hector,
She is a theme of honor and renown,
A spur to valiant and magnanimous deeds,
Whose present courage may beat down our foes
And fame in time to come canonize us ;
For I presume brave Hector would not lose
So rich advantage of a promised glory
As smiles upon the forehead of this action
For the wide world's revenue.

HECTOR   I am yours,
You valiant offspring of great Priamus.
I have a roisting challenge sent amongst   208
The dull and factious nobles of the Greeks
Will strike amazement to their drowsy spirits.
I was advertised their great general slept   211
Whilst emulation in the army crept.   212
This, I presume, will wake him.   *Exeunt.*

* * *

Enter Thersites solus.   II, iii

THERSITES How now, Thersites ? What, lost in the laby-
rinth of thy fury ? Shall the elephant Ajax carry it thus ? 2
He beats me, and I rail at him. O worthy satisfaction !
Would it were otherwise – that I could beat him, whilst
he railed at me. 'Sfoot, I'll learn to conjure and raise   5
devils, but I'll see some issue of my spiteful execrations. 6
Then there's Achilles, a rare enginer. If Troy be not
taken till these two undermine it, the walls will stand till
they fall of themselves. O thou great thunder-darter of

196 *heaving spleens* aroused passions 208 *roisting* roistering 211 *ad-
vertised* informed 212 *emulation* quarrelsome rivalry
II, iii Before the tent of Achilles 2 *carry it* carry off the honors 5
'Sfoot God's foot 6 *but I'll see* rather than not see

67

Olympus, forget that thou art Jove, the king of gods;
11   and, Mercury, lose all the serpentine craft of thy caduceus, if ye take not that little, little, less than little wit from
them that they have; which short-armed ignorance itself knows is so abundant scarce it will not in circum-
vention deliver a fly from a spider, without drawing their
massy irons and cutting the web. After this, the ven-
17   geance on the whole camp! or, rather, the Neapolitan
bone-ache, for that, methinks, is the curse depending on
19   those that war for a placket. I have said my prayers, and
devil Envy say 'Amen.' What ho, my Lord Achilles!
          Enter Patroclus.
PATROCLUS Who's there? Thersites? Good Thersites,
come in and rail.

THERSITES If I could 'a' remembered a gilt counterfeit,
24   thou wouldst not have slipped out of my contemplation.
But it is no matter; thyself upon thyself! The common
curse of mankind, folly and ignorance, be thine in great
27   revenue. Heaven bless thee from a tutor, and discipline
28   come not near thee. Let thy blood be thy direction till
thy death. Then, if she that lays thee out says thou art a
fair corse, I'll be sworn and sworn upon't she never
31   shrouded any but lazars. Amen. Where's Achilles?

PATROCLUS What, art thou devout? Wast thou in
prayer?

THERSITES Ay; the heavens hear me!

PATROCLUS Amen.
          Enter Achilles.
ACHILLES Who's there?

PATROCLUS Thersites, my lord.

ACHILLES Where, where, O, where? Art thou come?
Why, my cheese, my digestion, why hast thou not

---

11 *caduceus* Mercury's staff of office, twined with snakes   17–18 *Neapolitan bone-ache* syphilis   19 *placket* petticoat, i.e. woman   24 *slipped*
(pun on 'slip,' a counterfeit coin of brass covered with silver or gold)
27 *bless* save   28 *blood* violent passion   31 *lazars* lepers

served thyself in to my table so many meals? Come,
what's Agamemnon?

THERSITES Thy commander, Achilles. Then tell me,
Patroclus, what's Achilles?

PATROCLUS Thy lord, Thersites. Then tell me, I pray
thee, what's thyself?

THERSITES Thy knower, Patroclus. Then tell me, Patroclus, what art thou?

PATROCLUS Thou must tell that knowest.

ACHILLES O tell, tell.

THERSITES I'll decline the whole question. Agamemnon   49
commands Achilles, Achilles is my lord, I am Patroclus'
knower, and Patroclus is a fool.

[PATROCLUS You rascal!

THERSITES Peace, fool! I have not done.

ACHILLES He is a privileged man. Proceed, Thersites.

THERSITES Agamemnon is a fool, Achilles is a fool, Thersites is a fool, and, as aforesaid, Patroclus is a fool.]

ACHILLES Derive this; come.

THERSITES Agamemnon is a fool to offer to command
Achilles, Achilles is a fool to be commanded of Agamemnon, Thersites is a fool to serve such a fool, and
this Patroclus is a fool positive.

PATROCLUS Why am I a fool?

THERSITES Make that demand of the Creator. It suffices
me thou art. Look you, who comes here?

*Enter [at a distance] Agamemnon, Ulysses, Nestor,
Diomedes, Ajax, and Calchas.*

ACHILLES Come, Patroclus, I'll speak with nobody.
Come in with me, Thersites.   *Exit.*

THERSITES Here is such patchery, such juggling, and   67
such knavery. All the argument is a whore and a cuckold, a good quarrel to draw emulous factions and bleed
to death upon. [Now, the dry serpigo on the subject,   70
and war and lechery confound all!]   *[Exit.]*

---

49 *decline* go through (as in declining a noun)   **67** *patchery* roguery   **70**
serpigo impetigo or similar skin eruption

AGAMEMNON Where is Achilles?

PATROCLUS
Within his tent, but ill-disposed, my lord.

AGAMEMNON
Let it be known to him that we are here.
75   He shent our messengers, and we lay by
76   Our appertainings, visiting of him.
Let him be told so, lest perchance he think
78   We dare not move the question of our place
Or know not what we are.

PATROCLUS   I shall so say to him.   *[Exit.]*

ULYSSES We saw him at the opening of his tent. He is not sick.

AJAX Yes, lion-sick, sick of proud heart. You may call it melancholy if you will favor the man; but, by my head, 'tis pride. But why, why? Let him show us a cause. [A word, my lord.]

[Takes Agamemnon aside.]

NESTOR What moves Ajax thus to bay at him?

ULYSSES Achilles hath inveigled his fool from him.

NESTOR Who, Thersites?

ULYSSES He.

90   NESTOR Then will Ajax lack matter, if he have lost his argument.

ULYSSES No, you see, he is his argument that has his argument, Achilles.

94   NESTOR All the better; their fraction is more our wish
95   than their faction. But it was a strong composure a fool could disunite.

ULYSSES The amity that wisdom knits not, folly may easily untie.

[Enter Patroclus.]

. Here comes Patroclus.

NESTOR No Achilles with him?

75 *shent* reviled   76 *appertainings* rights of rank   78 *move . . . place* raise the question of our authority   90 *argument* subject matter   94 *fraction* break   95 *faction* union; *composure* union

70

ULYSSES
   The elephant hath joints, but none for courtesy.
   His legs are legs for necessity, not for flexure.   102

PATROCLUS
   Achilles bids me say, he is much sorry
   If anything more than your sport and pleasure
   Did move your greatness and this noble state   105
   To call upon him; he hopes it is no other
   But, for your health and your digestion sake,
   An after-dinner's breath.   108

AGAMEMNON   Hear you, Patroclus.
   We are too well acquainted with these answers;
   But his evasion, winged thus swift with scorn,
   Cannot outfly our apprehensions.
   Much attribute he hath, and much the reason
   Why we ascribe it to him; yet all his virtues,
   Not virtuously on his own part beheld,   114
   Do in our eyes begin to lose their gloss,
   Yea, like fair fruit in an unwholesome dish,
   Are like to rot untasted. Go and tell him,
   We come to speak with him; and you shall not sin
   If you do say we think him over-proud
   And under-honest, in self-assumption greater   120
   Than in the note of judgment; and worthier than   121
     himself
   Here tend the savage strangeness he puts on,   122
   Disguise the holy strength of their command,   123
   And underwrite in an observing kind
   His humorous predominance; yea, watch
   His course and time, his ebbs and flows, as if
   The passage and whole carriage of this action
   Rode on his tide. Go tell him this, and add

102 *flexure* bending   105 *state* accompanying noblemen   108 *breath* exercise   114 *Not . . . beheld* not modestly borne   120 *under-honest* lacking in open dealing   121 *note of judgment* esteem of men of judgment   122 *tend . . . strangeness* wait upon the rude aloofness   123–25 *Disguise . . . predominance* hide their god-given authority and acquiesce obediently in his eccentric claim to superiority

129   That, if he overhold his price so much,
130   We'll none of him; but let him, like an engine
      Not portable, lie under this report:
      'Bring action hither, this cannot go to war.'
133   A stirring dwarf we do allowance give
      Before a sleeping giant. Tell him so.

PATROCLUS
      I shall, and bring his answer presently.   [*Exit.*]

AGAMEMNON
      In second voice we'll not be satisfied;
      We come to speak with him. Ulysses, enter you.
                                                    [*Exit Ulysses.*]

AJAX   What is he more than another?

AGAMEMNON No more than what he thinks he is.

AJAX   Is he so much? Do you not think he thinks himself a
      better man than I am?

AGAMEMNON No question.

AJAX   Will you subscribe his thought, and say he is?

AGAMEMNON No, noble Ajax; you are as strong, as
      valiant, as wise, no less noble, much more gentle, and
      altogether more tractable.

AJAX   Why should a man be proud? How doth pride
      grow? I know not what pride is.

AGAMEMNON Your mind is the clearer and your virtues
      the fairer. He that is proud eats up himself. Pride is his
151   own glass, his own trumpet, his own chronicle; and
      whatever praises itself but in the deed, devours the
      deed in the praise.

AJAX   I do hate a proud man, as I do hate the engendering
      of toads.

NESTOR [*aside*] And yet he loves himself. Is't not strange?
                   Enter Ulysses.

ULYSSES
      Achilles will not to the field to-morrow.

---

129 *overhold* overvalue   130 *engine* mechanical contrivance (here military)
133 *allowance* approbation   151 *glass* mirror

AGAMEMNON
  What's his excuse?
ULYSSES   He doth rely on none,
  But carries on the stream of his dispose   158
  Without observance or respect of any,
  In will peculiar and in self-admission.   160
AGAMEMNON
  Why will he not upon our fair request
  Untent his person and share th' air with us?
ULYSSES
  Things small as nothing, for request's sake only, 163
  He makes important. Possessed he is with greatness,
  And speaks not to himself but with a pride
  That quarrels at self-breath. Imagined worth   166
  Holds in his blood such swoln and hot discourse
  That 'twixt his mental and his active parts
  Kingdomed Achilles in commotion rages   169
  And batters down himself. What should I say?
  He is so plaguy proud that the death-tokens of it 171
  Cry 'No recovery.'
AGAMEMNON   Let Ajax go to him.
  Dear lord, go you and greet him in his tent:
  'Tis said he holds you well, and will be led
  At your request a little from himself.
ULYSSES
  O Agamemnon, let it not be so!
  We'll consecrate the steps that Ajax makes
  When they go from Achilles. Shall the proud lord
  That bastes his arrogance with his own seam
  And never suffers matter of the world   179
  Enter his thoughts, save such as doth revolve
  And ruminate himself, shall he be worshipped

---

158 *dispose* bent of mind   160 *self-admission* self-approval   163 *for ... only* only because they are requested   166 *That ... self-breath* that quarrels with itself for speaking   169 *Kingdomed* i.e. Achilles is like a kingdom in civil war   171 *death-tokens* symptoms of the plague on the body   179 *seam* fat

Of that we hold an idol more than he?
No, this thrice-worthy and right valiant lord
185 Shall not so stale his palm, nobly acquired,
186 Nor, by my will, assubjugate his merit,
As amply titled as Achilles' is,
By going to Achilles.
That were to enlard his fat-already pride,
190 And add more coals to Cancer when he burns
191 With entertaining great Hyperion.
This lord go to him! Jupiter forbid,
And say in thunder, 'Achilles, go to him.'

NESTOR [aside]
194 O, this is well. He rubs the vein of him.

DIOMEDES [aside]
And how his silence drinks up his applause!

AJAX
If I go to him, with my armèd fist
197 I'll pash him o'er the face.

AGAMEMNON
O, no! you shall not go.

AJAX
199 An he be proud with me, I'll pheese his pride.
Let me go to him.

ULYSSES
Not for the worth that hangs upon our quarrel.

AJAX A paltry, insolent fellow!

NESTOR [aside] How he describes himself!

AJAX Can he not be sociable?

ULYSSES [aside] The raven chides blackness.

206 AJAX I'll let his humorous blood.

AGAMEMNON [aside] He will be the physician that should
be the patient.

---

185 *stale his palm* sully his glory   186 *assubjugate* debase   190 *Cancer* i.e.
summer, which begins under this sign of the Zodiac   191 *Hyperion* the
sun   194 *vein* mood   197 *pash* batter   199 *pheese* settle the matter of
206 *let ... blood* cure his humors by letting blood

AJAX An all men were of my mind –

ULYSSES *[aside]* Wit would be out of fashion.

AJAX 'A should not bear it so, 'a should eat swords first. 211
Shall pride carry it ?

NESTOR *[aside]* An 'twould, you'd carry half.

ULYSSES *[aside]* 'A would have ten shares.

AJAX I will knead him ; I'll make him supple.

NESTOR *[aside]* He's not yet through warm. Force him 216
with praises ; pour in, pour in ; his ambition is dry.

ULYSSES *[to Agamemnon]*
My lord, you feed too much on this dislike.

NESTOR
Our noble general, do not do so.

DIOMEDES
You must prepare to fight without Achilles.

ULYSSES
Why, 'tis this naming of him does him harm.
Here is a man – but 'tis before his face ;
I will be silent.

NESTOR   Wherefore should you so ?
He is not emulous, as Achilles is.   224

ULYSSES
Know the whole world, he is as valiant –

AJAX
A whoreson dog, that shall palter with us thus !   226
Would he were a Troyan !

NESTOR What a vice were it in Ajax now –

ULYSSES If he were proud –

DIOMEDES Or covetous of praise –

ULYSSES Ay, or surly borne –

DIOMEDES Or strange, or self-affected !   232

ULYSSES
Thank the heavens, lord, thou art of sweet composure ;
Praise him that got thee, she that gave thee suck ;

211 *'A* he 216 *through* thoroughly 224 *emulous* envious 226 *palter*
dodge 232 *strange, or self-affected* distant or caring only for himself

Famed be thy tutor, and thy parts of nature
236   Thrice-famed beyond all erudition;
But he that disciplined thine arms to fight,
Let Mars divide eternity in twain
And give him half; and, for thy vigor,
240   Bull-bearing Milo his addition yield
To sinewy Ajax. I will not praise thy wisdom,
242   Which, like a bourn, a pale, a shore, confines
Thy spacious and dilated parts. Here's Nestor,
244   Instructed by the antiquary times,
He must, he is, he cannot but be wise;
But pardon, father Nestor, were your days
As green as Ajax, and your brain so tempered,
You should not have the eminence of him,
But be as Ajax.

AJAX   Shall I call you father?

NESTOR
Ay, my good son.

DIOMEDES   Be ruled by him, Lord Ajax.

ULYSSES
There is no tarrying here; the hart Achilles
Keeps thicket. Please it our great general
253   To call together all his state of war;
Fresh kings are come to Troy. To-morrow,
255   We must with all our main of power stand fast.
And here's a lord – come knights from east to west,
And cull their flower, Ajax shall cope the best.

AGAMEMNON
Go we to council. Let Achilles sleep:
Light boats sail swift, though greater hulks draw deep.
                                        Exeunt.

*

236 *erudition* knowledge   240 *Milo* a famous Greek athlete; *addition* i.e. his
epithet (*Bull-bearing*)   242 *bourn* boundary; *pale* fence   244 *antiquary* i.e.
studied by antiquaries   253 *state* nobles in council   255 *main* might of
military power

*[Music sounds within.] Enter Pandarus [and a
  Servant].*   III, i

PANDARUS Friend you, pray you a word. Do you not follow the young Lord Paris?

SERVANT Ay, sir, when he goes before me.

PANDARUS You depend upon him, I mean.   4

SERVANT Sir, I do depend upon the Lord.

PANDARUS You depend upon a noble gentleman; I must
  needs praise him.

SERVANT The Lord be praised!

PANDARUS You know me, do you not?

SERVANT Faith, sir, superficially.

PANDARUS Friend, know me better. I am the Lord Pandarus.

SERVANT I hope I shall know your honor better.

PANDARUS I do desire it.

SERVANT You are in the state of grace.   14

PANDARUS Grace? Not so, friend. Honor and lordship   15
  are my titles. What music is this?

SERVANT I do but partly know, sir. It is music in parts.

PANDARUS Know you the musicians?

SERVANT Wholly, sir.

PANDARUS Who play they to?

SERVANT To the hearers, sir.

PANDARUS At whose pleasure, friend?

SERVANT At mine, sir, and theirs that love music.

PANDARUS Command, I mean, friend.

SERVANT Who shall I command, sir?

PANDARUS Friend, we understand not one another. I am
  too courtly, and thou too cunning. At whose request do
  these men play?

SERVANT That's to't, indeed, sir. Marry, sir, at the request of Paris, my lord, who is there in person; with him   30

III, i The palace of Priam 4 *depend* are in a position of dependence
14 *You . . . grace* (he pretends that Pandarus meant 'I desire to be better')
15 *Grace* the title of a duke, etc.

77

the mortal Venus, the heart-blood of beauty, love's in-
visible soul.

PANDARUS Who? My cousin Cressida?

SERVANT No, sir, Helen. Could you not find out that by
her attributes?

PANDARUS It should seem, fellow, that thou hast not
seen the Lady Cressid. I come to speak with Paris from
the Prince Troilus. I will make a complimental assault
39 upon him, for my business seethes.

40 SERVANT Sodden business! There's a stewed phrase, indeed.

Enter Paris and Helen.

PANDARUS Fair be to you, my lord, and to all this fair
company. Fair desires in all fair measure fairly guide
43 them. Especially to you, fair queen, fair thoughts be
your fair pillow.

HELEN Dear lord, you are full of fair words.

PANDARUS You speak your fair pleasure, sweet queen.
47 Fair prince, here is good broken music.

PARIS You have broke it, cousin; and, by my life, you
shall make it whole again; you shall piece it out with a
piece of your performance. Nell, he is full of harmony.

PANDARUS Truly, lady, no.

HELEN O, sir!

PANDARUS Rude, in sooth; in good sooth, very rude.

54 PARIS Well said, my lord. Well, you say so in fits.

PANDARUS I have business to my lord, dear queen. My
lord, will you vouchsafe me a word?

57 HELEN Nay, this shall not hedge us out. We'll hear you
sing, certainly.

PANDARUS Well, sweet queen, you are pleasant with me.
But, marry, thus, my lord: my dear lord and most esteemed friend, your brother Troilus –

39 *seethes* is at full boil, i.e. in haste   40 *stewed* (1) boiled, (2) pertaining to
stews (brothels)   43 *queen* possible quibble on 'quean': slut (Helen was
queen to Menelaus, not to Paris)   47 *broken music* music by a group of
different instruments   54 *fits* parts of a song   57 *hedge* shut

78

HELEN My Lord Pandarus, honey-sweet lord –

PANDARUS Go to, sweet queen, go to – commends himself most affectionately to you.

HELEN You shall not bob us out of our melody. If you do, 65
our melancholy upon your head!

PANDARUS Sweet queen, sweet queen; that's a sweet queen, i' faith.

HELEN And to make a sweet lady sad is a sour offense.

PANDARUS Nay, that shall not serve your turn; that shall it not, in truth, la. Nay, I care not for such words; no, no. And, my lord, he desires you that, if the king call for him at supper, you will make his excuse.

HELEN My Lord Pandarus –

PANDARUS What says my sweet queen, my very, very sweet queen?

PARIS What exploit's in hand? Where sups he to-night?

HELEN Nay, but my lord –

PANDARUS What says my sweet queen? My cousin will fall out with you.

HELEN You must not know where he sups.

PARIS I'll lay my life, with my disposer Cressida.   82

PANDARUS No, no; no such matter; you are wide. Come, 83
your disposer is sick.

PARIS Well, I'll make excuse.

PANDARUS Ay, good my lord. Why should you say Cressida? No, your poor disposer's sick.

PARIS I spy.

PANDARUS You spy? What do you spy? Come, give me an instrument now, sweet queen.

HELEN Why, this is kindly done.

PANDARUS My niece is horribly in love with a thing you have, sweet queen.

HELEN She shall have it, my lord, if it be not my Lord Paris.

---

65 *bob* cheat   82 *my disposer* i.e. who manages me   83 *wide* wide of the mark

PANDARUS He? No, she'll none of him; they two are
95   twain.

HELEN Falling in, after falling out, may make them three.

PANDARUS Come, come, I'll hear no more of this. I'll
   sing you a song now.

HELEN Ay, ay, prithee. Now by my troth, sweet lord,
   thou hast a fine forehead.

101 PANDARUS Ay, you may, you may.

HELEN Let thy song be love. This love will undo us all.
   O Cupid, Cupid, Cupid!

PANDARUS Love! ay, that it shall, i' faith.

PARIS Ay, good, now 'Love, love, nothing but love.'

PANDARUS [In good troth, it begins so :]
     [Sings.]
    Love, love, nothing but love, still love still more!
    For, O, love's bow shoots buck and doe.
    The shaft confounds not that it wounds,
110   But tickles still the sore.
    These lovers cry, O ho! they die!
    Yet that which seems the wound to kill
    Doth turn O ho! to Ha, ha, he!
    So dying love lives still.
    O ho! a while, but Ha, ha, ha!
    O ho! groans out for Ha, ha, ha! – Heigh ho!

HELEN In love, i' faith, to the very tip of the nose.

PARIS He eats nothing but doves, love, and that breeds
   hot blood, and hot blood begets hot thoughts, and hot
120   thoughts beget hot deeds, and hot deeds is love.

PANDARUS Is this the generation of love – hot blood, hot
   thoughts, and hot deeds? Why, they are vipers. Is love a
   generation of vipers? Sweet lord, who's a-field to-day?

PARIS Hector, Deiphobus, Helenus, Antenor, and all the
   gallantry of Troy. I would fain have armed to-day, but
   my Nell would not have it so. How chance my brother
   Troilus went not?

95 *twain* at odds   **101** *you may* i.e. have your joke   **110** *sore* wound, or
buck of fourth year

HELEN He hangs the lip at something. You know all,
  Lord Pandarus.

PANDARUS Not I, honey-sweet queen. I long to hear how *130*
  they sped to-day. You'll remember your brother's excuse?

PARIS To a hair.

PANDARUS Farewell, sweet queen.

HELEN Commend me to your niece.

PANDARUS I will, sweet queen. *[Exit.] Sound a retreat.*

PARIS
  They're come from the field. Let us to Priam's hall
  To greet the warriors. Sweet Helen, I must woo you
  To help unarm our Hector. His stubborn buckles,
  With these your white enchanting fingers touched,
  Shall more obey than to the edge of steel
  Or force of Greekish sinews. You shall do more
  Than all the island kings – disarm great Hector. *143*

HELEN
  'Twill make us proud to be his servant, Paris;
  Yea, what he shall receive of us in duty
  Gives us more palm in beauty than we have,
  Yea, overshines ourself.

PARIS
  Sweet, above thought I love thee. *Exeunt.*

*

Enter Pandarus [and] Troilus' Man. III, ii

PANDARUS How now, where's thy master? At my cousin
  Cressida's?

MAN No, sir; he stays for you to conduct him thither.
  [Enter Troilus.]

PANDARUS O, here he comes. How now, how now?

TROILUS Sirrah, walk off. *[Exit Man.]*

143 *island* i.e. Greek
III, ii Pandarus' orchard

PANDARUS Have you seen my cousin ?

TROILUS

No, Pandarus. I stalk about her door

8   Like a strange soul upon the Stygian banks

9   Staying for waftage. O, be thou my Charon,
And give me swift transportation to those fields
Where I may wallow in the lily-beds

12   Proposed for the deserver. O gentle Pandar,
From Cupid's shoulder pluck his painted wings,
And fly with me to Cressid.

PANDARUS

15   Walk here i' th' orchard. I'll bring her straight.   *[Exit.]*

TROILUS

I am giddy ; expectation whirls me round.
Th' imaginary relish is so sweet
That it enchants my sense. What will it be

19   When that the wat'ry palates taste indeed
Love's thrice-repurèd nectar ? Death, I fear me,

21   Sounding destruction, or some joy too fine,
Too subtle, potent, tuned too sharp in sweetness
For the capacity of my ruder powers.
I fear it much ; and I do fear besides

25   That I shall lose distinction in my joys,
As doth a battle, when they charge on heaps
The enemy flying.
[Enter Pandarus.]

PANDARUS She's making her ready ; she'll come straight ;

29   you must be witty now. She does so blush, and fetches

30   her wind so short as if she were frayed with a spirit. I'll

31   fetch her. It is the prettiest villain ; she fetches her
breath as short as a new-ta'en sparrow.   *[Exit.]*

---

8 *Stygian* (the Styx was a river of the underworld) 9 *waftage* passage
by water; *Charon* ferryman of the dead across the Styx to Hades 12
Proposed promised 15 *orchard* garden 19 *wat'ry* watering (cf. 'mouth
waters') 21 *Sounding* swooning 25 *distinction* power of distinguishing
29 *be witty* have your wits about you 30 *frayed with a spirit* frightened
by a ghost 31 *villain* (a term of endearment here)

TROILUS
   Even such a passion doth embrace my bosom.
   My heart beats thicker than a feverous pulse,
   And all my powers do their bestowing lose,   35
   Like vassalage at unawares encount'ring   36
   The eye of majesty.
    Enter Pandarus and Cressida.

PANDARUS Come, come, what need you blush? Shame's
a baby. Here she is now; swear the oaths now to her that
you have sworn to me. What! are you gone again? You
must be watched ere you be made tame, must you? 41
Come your ways, come your ways; an you draw backward, we'll put you i' th' fills. Why do you not speak to 43
her? Come, draw this curtain, and let's see your picture. 44
Alas the day, how loath you are to offend daylight! An
'twere dark, you'd close sooner. So, so; rub on, and kiss 46
the mistress. How now, a kiss in fee-farm! Build there, 47
carpenter; the air is sweet. Nay, you shall fight your
hearts out ere I part you. The falcon as the tercel, for all 49
the ducks i' th' river. Go to, go to.

TROILUS You have bereft me of all words, lady.

PANDARUS Words pay no debts, give her deeds; but
she'll bereave you o' th' deeds too if she call your activity
in question. What, billing again? Here's 'In witness 54
whereof the parties interchangeably' – Come in, come
in. I'll go get a fire.   *[Exit.]*

CRESSIDA Will you walk in, my lord?

TROILUS O Cressid, how often have I wished me thus!

CRESSIDA Wished, my lord? The gods grant – O my lord!

TROILUS What should they grant? What makes this

---

35 *bestowing* proper use   **36** *vassalage* vassals   **41** *watched* kept awake (a
method used in taming a hawk)   **43** *fills* shafts   **44** *curtain* i.e. veil
46–47 *rub . . . mistress* (in bowling, 'to rub' was to meet obstacles in the
way of the object-ball or 'mistress')   **47** *in fee-farm* in perpetuity   **49–50**
The falcon . . . river i.e. I will bet on the falcon (female hawk, i.e. Cressida)
against the tercel (male hawk) to bring down any amount of game   **54–55**
In witness . . . interchangeably (a legal formula completed by the words
'have set their hands and seals')

61   pretty abruption? What too curious dreg espies my
sweet lady in the fountain of our love?

CRESSIDA More dregs than water, if my fears have eyes.

TROILUS Fears make devils of cherubins; they never see
truly.

CRESSIDA Blind fear, that seeing reason leads, finds safer
footing than blind reason stumbling without fear. To
fear the worst oft cures the worse.

TROILUS O, let my lady apprehend no fear. In all Cupid's
pageant there is presented no monster.

70 CRESSIDA Nor nothing monstrous neither?

TROILUS Nothing but our undertakings when we vow to
weep seas, live in fire, eat rocks, tame tigers, thinking it
harder for our mistress to devise imposition enough
than for us to undergo any difficulty imposed. This is
the monstruosity in love, lady, that the will is infinite
and the execution confined; that the desire is boundless
and the act a slave to limit.

CRESSIDA They say all lovers swear more performance
than they are able, and yet reserve an ability that they
never perform, vowing more than the perfection of ten
and discharging less than the tenth part of one. They
that have the voice of lions and the act of hares, are they
not monsters?

TROILUS Are there such? Such are not we. Praise us as
85   we are tasted, allow us as we prove; our head shall go
86   bare till merit crown it. No perfection in reversion shall
have a praise in present; we will not name desert before
his birth, and, being born, his addition shall be humble.
Few words to fair faith. Troilus shall be such to Cressid,
90   as what envy can say worst shall be a mock for his truth,
and what truth can speak truest not truer than Troilus.

CRESSIDA Will you walk in, my lord?

---

61 *abruption* breaking off; *curious* causing care or anxiety   85 *tasted* tested;
allow approve   86 *reversion* right of future possession   90 *as what . . . truth*
that malice can say no worse than to sneer at his constancy

Enter Pandarus.

PANDARUS What, blushing still? Have you not done
  talking yet?

CRESSIDA Well, uncle, what folly I commit, I dedicate to
  you.

PANDARUS I thank you for that. If my lord get a boy of
  you, you'll give him me. Be true to my lord; if he flinch,
  chide me for it.

TROILUS You know now your hostages, your uncle's   *100*
  word and my firm faith.

PANDARUS Nay, I'll give my word for her too. Our
  kindred, though they be long ere they be wooed, they
  are constant being won. They are burrs, I can tell you;
  they'll stick where they are thrown.

CRESSIDA
  Boldness comes to me now and brings me heart.
  Prince Troilus, I have loved you night and day
  For many weary months.

TROILUS
  Why was my Cressid then so hard to win?

CRESSIDA
  Hard to seem won; but I was won, my lord,   *110*
  With the first glance that ever – pardon me:
  If I confess much you will play the tyrant.
  I love you now, but not, till now, so much
  But I might master it. In faith, I lie;
  My thoughts were like unbridled children grown
  Too headstrong for their mother. See, we fools!
  Why have I blabbed? Who shall be true to us
  When we are so unsecret to ourselves?
  But, though I loved you well, I wooed you not;
  And yet, good faith, I wished myself a man,   *120*
  Or that we women had men's privilege
  Of speaking first. Sweet, bid me hold my tongue,
  For in this rapture I shall surely speak
  The thing I shall repent. See, see! your silence,
  Cunning in dumbness, from my weakness draws

126 My very soul of counsel. Stop my mouth.

TROILUS
And shall, albeit sweet music issues thence.

PANDARUS Pretty, i' faith.

CRESSIDA
My lord, I do beseech you, pardon me ;
'Twas not my purpose thus to beg a kiss.
I am ashamed. O heavens, what have I done ?
For this time will I take my leave, my lord.

TROILUS
Your leave, sweet Cressid ?

PANDARUS Leave! An you take leave till to-morrow
morning –

CRESSIDA
Pray you, content you.

TROILUS   What offends you, lady ?

CRESSIDA
Sir, mine own company.

TROILUS
You cannot shun yourself.

CRESSIDA
Let me go and try.
I have a kind of self resides with you ;
But an unkind self, that itself will leave
142 To be another's fool. I would be gone.
Where is my wit ? I know not what I speak.

TROILUS
Well know they what they speak that speak so wisely.

CRESSIDA
Perchance, my lord, I show more craft than love,
146 And fell so roundly to a large confession
147 To angle for your thoughts. But you are wise,

---

126 *soul of counsel* inmost secrets   142 *fool* dupe   146 *roundly* straight-
forwardly; *large* unrestrained   147–49 *But . . . might* (either the text is
corrupt or Cressida contradicts herself)

Or else you love not, for to be wise and love
Exceeds man's might; that dwells with gods above.

TROILUS

O! that I thought it could be in a woman –
As, if it can, I will presume in you –
To feed for aye her lamp and flames of love;
To keep her constancy in plight and youth,   153
Outliving beauty's outward, with a mind
That doth renew swifter than blood decays;
Or that persuasion could but thus convince me
That my integrity and truth to you
Might be affronted with the match and weight   158
Of such a winnowed purity in love;
How were I then uplifted! But, alas,
I am as true as truth's simplicity,
And simpler than the infancy of truth.

CRESSIDA

In that I'll war with you.

TROILUS   O virtuous fight,
When right with right wars who shall be most right!
True swains in love shall in the world to come
Approve their truth by Troilus. When their rhymes,   166
Full of protest, of oath, and big compare,
Wants similes, truth tired with iteration,
'As true as steel, as plantage to the moon,   169
As sun to day, as turtle to her mate,   170
As iron to adamant, as earth to th' centre,'   171
Yet, after all comparisons of truth,
As truth's authentic author to be cited,
'As true as Troilus' shall crown up the verse
And sanctify the numbers.   175

CRESSIDA   Prophet may you be!

153 *in plight and youth* as it was plighted, and as fresh   158 *affronted*
confronted   166 *Approve* attest   169 *plantage* vegetation (the moon was
supposed to influence vegetation)   170 *turtle* turtledove (a type of love
faithful to death)   171 *adamant* loadstone (magnetic)   175 *numbers* verses

If I be false or swerve a hair from truth,
When time is old and hath forgot itself,
When waterdrops have worn the stones of Troy,
And blind oblivion swallowed cities up,
180 And mighty states characterless are grated
To dusty nothing, yet let memory,
From false to false among false maids in love,
Upbraid my falsehood! When th' have said, 'as false
As air, as water, wind or sandy earth,
As fox to lamb, as wolf to heifer's calf,
186 Pard to the hind, or stepdame to her son,'
Yea, let them say, to stick the heart of falsehood,
'As false as Cressid.'

PANDARUS Go to, a bargain made; seal it, seal it; I'll be
the witness. Here I hold your hand, here my cousin's. If
ever you prove false one to another, since I have taken
such pains to bring you together, let all pitiful goers-
between be called to the world's end after my name; call
194 them all Pandars; let all constant men be Troiluses, all
false women Cressids, and all brokers-between Pandars! Say, 'Amen.'

TROILUS Amen.

CRESSIDA Amen.

PANDARUS Amen. Whereupon I will show you a cham-
199 ber which bed, because it shall not speak of your pretty
encounters, press it to death. Away!

Exeunt [Troilus and Cressida].

And Cupid grant all tongue-tied maidens here
Bed, chamber, Pandar to provide this gear!   *Exit.*

*

---

180 *characterless* without a mark   186 *Pard* panther or leopard; *hind* doe
194 *constant* (the context demands 'inconstant,' but the text foretells the
outcome of the play)   199 *which bed* in which the bed; *because* in order that

[Flourish of trumpets.] Enter Ulysses, Diomedes,   III, iii
Nestor, Agamemnon, [Menelaus, Ajax, and]
Calchas.

CALCHAS

Now, princes, for the service I have done,
Th' advantage of the time prompts me aloud
To call for recompense. Appear it to mind
That through the sight I bear in things to love,
I have abandoned Troy, left my possession,   5
Incurred a traitor's name, exposed myself,
From certain and possessed conveniences,
To doubtful fortunes, sequest'ring from me all   8
That time, acquaintance, custom, and condition
Made tame and most familiar to my nature;   10
And here, to do you service, am become
As new into the world, strange, unacquainted.
I do beseech you, as in way of taste,   13
To give me now a little benefit
Out of those many regist'red in promise,
Which, you say, live to come in my behalf.

AGAMEMNON

What wouldst thou of us, Troyan? Make demand.

CALCHAS

You have a Troyan prisoner, called Antenor,
Yesterday took; Troy holds him very dear.
Oft have you – often have you thanks therefor –
Desired my Cressid in right great exchange,   21
Whom Troy hath still denied; but this Antenor
I know is such a wrest in their affairs   23
That their negotiations all must slack,
Wanting his manage; and they will almost
Give us a prince of blood, a son of Priam,
In change of him. Let him be sent, great princes,

III, iii The Grecian camp **5** *abandoned* (cf. I, i, 77) **8** *sequest'ring*
putting away **10** *tame* familiar **13** *taste* foretaste **21** *right great exchange* exchange for someone very great **23** *wrest* key for tuning a harp,
i.e. key to harmony in Troy

And he shall buy my daughter; and her presence
Shall quite strike off all service I have done
30   In most accepted pain.
AGAMEMNON   Let Diomedes bear him,
And bring us Cressid hither. Calchas shall have
What he requests of us. Good Diomed,
Furnish you fairly for his interchange.
Withal bring word if Hector will to-morrow
Be answered in his challenge. Ajax is ready.

DIOMEDES
This shall I undertake, and 'tis a burden
Which I am proud to bear.   *Exit [with Calchas].*
     Achilles and Patroclus stand in their tent.

ULYSSES
Achilles stands i' th' entrance of his tent.
Please it our general to pass strangely by him,
As if he were forgot; and, princes all,
Lay negligent and loose regard upon him.
I will come last. 'Tis like he'll question me
43   Why such unplausive eyes are bent, why turned, on him.
If so, I have derision med'cinable
To use between your strangeness and his pride,
Which his own will shall have desire to drink.
It may do good; pride hath no other glass
48   To show itself but pride, for supple knees
Feed arrogance and are the proud man's fees.

AGAMEMNON
We'll execute your purpose, and put on
A form of strangeness as we pass along.
So do each lord, and either greet him not
Or else disdainfully, which shall shake him more
Than if not looked on. I will lead the way.

ACHILLES
What comes the general to speak with me?
You know my mind; I'll fight no more 'gainst Troy.

---

30 *accepted* cheerfully endured   43 *unplausive* disapproving   48 *show* mirror

AGAMEMNON
    What says Achilles? Would he aught with us?
NESTOR
    Would you, my lord, aught with the general?
ACHILLES No.
NESTOR Nothing, my lord.   60
AGAMEMNON The better.
ACHILLES Good day, good day.
MENELAUS How do you? How do you?
ACHILLES What, does the cuckold scorn me?
AJAX How now, Patroclus?
ACHILLES Good morrow, Ajax.
AJAX Ha?
ACHILLES Good morrow.
AJAX Ay, and good next day too.   *Exeunt.*
ACHILLES
    What mean these fellows? Know they not Achilles?   70
PATROCLUS
    They pass by strangely. They were used to bend,
    To send their smiles before them to Achilles,
    To come as humbly as they used to creep
    To holy altars.
ACHILLES   What, am I poor of late?
    'Tis certain, greatness, once fall'n out with fortune,
    Must fall out with men too. What the declined is
    He shall as soon read in the eyes of others
    As feel in his own fall; for men, like butterflies,
    Show not their mealy wings but to the summer,   79
    And not a man, for being simply man,
    Hath any honor, but honor for those honors
    That are without him, as place, riches, and favor,   82
    Prizes of accident as oft as merit;
    Which when they fall, as being slippery standers,
    The love that leaned on them as slippery too,
    Doth one pluck down another, and together

79 *mealy* powdered   82 *without* external to

91

Die in the fall. But 'tis not so with me ;
Fortune and I are friends. I do enjoy
89   At ample point all that I did possess,
Save these men's looks ; who do, methinks, find out
Something not worth in me such rich beholding
As they have often given. Here is Ulysses ;
I'll interrupt his reading.
How now, Ulysses.

ULYSSES   Now, great Thetis' son.

ACHILLES
What are you reading ?

ULYSSES   A strange fellow here
96   Writes me that man, how dearly ever parted,
97   How much in having, or without or in,
Cannot make boast to have that which he hath,
99   Nor feels not what he owes but by reflection ;
As when his virtues aiming upon others
Heat them, and they retort that heat again
To the first giver.

ACHILLES   This is not strange, Ulysses.
The beauty that is borne here in the face
The bearer knows not, but commends itself
To others' eyes ; nor doth the eye itself,
That most pure spirit of sense, behold itself,
Not going from itself ; but eye to eye opposed
Salutes each other with each other's form ;
109   For speculation turns not to itself
Till it hath travelled and is married there
Where it may see itself. This is not strange at all.

ULYSSES
112   I do not strain at the position,
It is familiar, but at the author's drift ;

89 *At ample point* in full measure   96 *how . . . parted* with however valuable
parts (i.e. natural endowments)   97 *having* possession; *or . . . in* external
or internal   99 *Nor . . . reflection* and perceives what he owns only as it is
reflected   109 *speculation* the power of sight   112 *position* i.e. of the writer
mentioned above

Who in his circumstance expressly proves 114
That no man is the lord of anything –
Though in and of him there be much consisting – 116
Till he communicate his parts to others ;
Nor doth he of himself know them for aught
Till he behold them formèd in th' applause
Where th' are extended ; who, like an arch, reverb'rate 120
The voice again, or, like a gate of steel
Fronting the sun, receives and renders back
His figure and his heat. I was much rapt in this,
And apprehended here immediately
Th' unknown Ajax.
Heavens, what a man is there ! A very horse,
That has he knows not what. Nature, what things there
    are
Most abject in regard and dear in use ! 128
What things again most dear in the esteem
And poor in worth ! Now shall we see to-morrow,
An act that very chance doth throw upon him,
Ajax renowned. O heavens, what some men do,
While some men leave to do !
How some men creep in skittish Fortune's hall, 134
Whiles others play the idiots in her eyes !
How one man eats into another's pride,
While pride is fasting in his wantonness ! 137
To see these Grecian lords – why, even already
They clap the lubber Ajax on the shoulder,
As if his foot were on brave Hector's breast,
And great Troy shrinking.

CHILLES

I do believe it ; for they passed by me
As misers do by beggars, neither gave to me
Good word nor look. What, are my deeds forgot ?

14 *in his circumstance* in getting down to details   116 *Though . . . consisting*
1ough much exists in him and because of him   120 *Where th' are extended*
which they are noised abroad; *who* which   128 *regard* esteem   134 *in*
to   137 *his wantonness* its own wanton self-satisfaction

ULYSSES

  Time hath, my lord, a wallet at his back,
  Wherein he puts alms for oblivion,
  A great-sized monster of ingratitudes.
  Those scraps are good deeds past, which are devoured
  As fast as they are made, forgot as soon
  As done. Perseverance, dear my lord,
  Keeps honor bright; to have done, is to hang
152 Quite out of fashion, like a rusty mail
153 In monumental mock'ry. Take the instant way;
  For honor travels in a strait so narrow
  Where one but goes abreast. Keep, then, the path;
  For emulation hath a thousand sons
  That one by one pursue. If you give way,
158 Or hedge aside from the direct forthright,
  Like to an ent'red tide they all rush by
  And leave you hindmost;
  [Or, like a gallant horse fall'n in first rank,
162 Lie there for pavement to the abject rear,
  O'errun and trampled on.] Then what they do in present,
  Though less than yours in past, must o'ertop yours;
  For time is like a fashionable host,
  That slightly shakes his parting guest by th' hand,
  And with his arms outstretched, as he would fly,
  Grasps in the comer. The welcome ever smiles,
  And farewell goes out sighing. Let not virtue seek
  Remuneration for the thing it was. For beauty, wit,
  High birth, vigor of bone, desert in service,
  Love, friendship, charity, are subjects all
  To envious and calumniating time.
174 One touch of nature makes the whole world kin,
175 That all with one consent praise new-born gawds,
  Though they are made and moulded of things past,

---

152 *mail* armor 153 *instant* immediately ahead 158 *forthright* straight
ahead 162 *abject rear* miserable specimens in the rear 174 *One touch of
nature* one common weakness, namely, praising *new-born gawds* 175
gawds toys, gewgaws

And give to dust that is a little gilt
More laud than gilt o'er-dusted.
The present eye praises the present object.
Then marvel not, thou great and complete man,
That all the Greeks begin to worship Ajax;
Since things in motion sooner catch the eye
Than what not stirs. The cry went once on thee,   183
And still it might, and yet it may again,
If thou wouldst not entomb thyself alive
And case thy reputation in thy tent;
Whose glorious deeds, but in these fields of late,
Made emulous missions 'mongst the gods themselves   188
And drave great Mars to faction.   189

ACHILLES   Of this my privacy
I have strong reasons.

ULYSSES   But 'gainst your privacy
The reasons are more potent and heroical.
'Tis known, Achilles, that you are in love
With one of Priam's daughters.   193

ACHILLES Ha! known!

ULYSSES
Is that a wonder?
The providence that's in a watchful state   196
Knows almost every grain of Pluto's gold,   197
Finds bottom in th' uncomprehensive deeps,   198
Keeps place with thought, and almost, like the gods,
Does thoughts unveil in their dumb cradles.
There is a mystery – with whom relation   201
Durst never meddle – in the soul of state,
Which hath an operation more divine
Than breath or pen can give expressure to.

---

183 *cry* public acclaim   188 *emulous missions* (the gods joined in the fighting,
taking opposing sides)   189 *to faction* to become a partisan   193 *one . . .
daughters* Polyxena (with whom, in one legend, Achilles was keeping a
tryst when Paris shot him in his vulnerable heel)   196 *providence* (here,
timely care rather than foresight)   197 *Pluto's* (Shakespeare confused
Pluto, god of the underworld, with Plutus, god of wealth)   198 *uncomprehensive* unfathomable   201 *relation* open statement

All the commerce that you have had with Troy
As perfectly is ours as yours, my lord;
And better would it fit Achilles much
To throw down Hector than Polyxena.
209 But it must grieve young Pyrrhus now at home,
When fame shall in our islands sound her trump,
And all the Greekish girls shall tripping sing,
'Great Hector's sister did Achilles win,
But our great Ajax bravely beat down him.'
Farewell, my lord; I as your lover speak;
The fool slides o'er the ice that you should break.   *[Exit.]*

PATROCLUS
To this effect, Achilles, have I moved you.
A woman impudent and mannish grown
Is not more loathed than an effeminate man
In time of action. I stand condemned for this.
They think my little stomach to the war
And your great love to me restrains you thus.
Sweet, rouse yourself; and the weak wanton Cupid
Shall from your neck unloose his amorous fold
And, like a dew-drop from the lion's mane,
Be shook to air.

ACHILLES   Shall Ajax fight with Hector?

PATROCLUS
Ay, and perhaps receive much honor by him.

ACHILLES
I see my reputation is at stake;
228 My fame is shrewdly gored.

PATROCLUS   O, then, beware!
Those wounds heal ill that men do give themselves.
Omission to do what is necessary
231 Seals a commission to a blank of danger;

---

209 *Pyrrhus* son of Achilles (also called Neoptolemus), who came to the siege after his father's death   **228** *shrewdly gored* seriously wounded   **231** *Seals . . . danger* binds one to encounter unknown dangers (royal agents were given blank commissions, already sealed, to use for arrests or exactions)

And danger, like an ague, subtly taints
Even then when we sit idly in the sun.

ACHILLES
Go call Thersites hither, sweet Patroclus.
I'll send the fool to Ajax and desire him
T' invite the Troyan lords after the combat
To see us here unarmed. I have a woman's longing,   237
An appetite that I am sick withal,
To see great Hector in his weeds of peace,   239
To talk with him and to behold his visage,
Even to my full of view. A labor saved!
    Enter Thersites.

THERSITES A wonder!

ACHILLES What?

THERSITES Ajax goes up and down the field, asking for
himself.   245

ACHILLES How so?

THERSITES He must fight singly to-morrow with Hector, and is so prophetically proud of an heroical
cudgelling that he raves in saying nothing.

ACHILLES How can that be?

THERSITES Why, 'a stalks up and down like a peacock – a
stride and a stand; ruminates like an hostess that hath no
arithmetic but her brain to set down her reckoning; bites
his lip with a politic regard, as who should say, 'There   254
were wit in this head an 'twould out'; and so there is,
but it lies as coldly in him as fire in a flint, which will not
show without knocking. The man's undone for ever, for
if Hector break not his neck i' th' combat, he'll break't
himself in vainglory. He knows not me. I said, 'Good
morrow, Ajax'; and he replies, 'Thanks, Agamemnon.'
What think you of this man that takes me for the
general? He's grown a very land-fish, languageless, a
monster. A plague of opinion! A man may wear it on

---

237 *woman's* i.e. pregnant woman's   **239** *weeds* dress   **245** *himself* ('Ajax,'
i.e. a jakes, was slang for a privy)   **254** *politic regard* expression of wisdom

264   both sides like a leather jerkin.

ACHILLES Thou must be my ambassador to him, Thersites.

THERSITES Who, I? Why, he'll answer nobody; he professes not answering. Speaking is for beggars; he wears
268   his tongue in's arms. I will put on his presence; let Patroclus make demands to me, you shall see the pageant of Ajax.

ACHILLES To him, Patroclus. Tell him I humbly desire the valiant Ajax to invite the most valorous Hector to come unarmed to my tent, and to procure safe-conduct for his person of the magnanimous and most illustrious, six-or-seven-times-honored captain-general of the Grecian army, Agamemnon, et caetera. Do this.

PATROCLUS Jove bless great Ajax!

THERSITES Hum!

PATROCLUS I come from the worthy Achilles –

THERSITES Ha!

280   PATROCLUS Who most humbly desires you to invite Hector to his tent –

THERSITES Hum!

PATROCLUS And to procure safe-conduct from Agamemnon.

THERSITES Agamemnon?

PATROCLUS Ay, my lord.

THERSITES Ha!

PATROCLUS What say you to't?

THERSITES God be wi' you, with all my heart.

PATROCLUS Your answer, sir.

290   THERSITES If to-morrow be a fair day, by eleven of the clock it will be one way or other; howsoever, he shall pay for me ere he has me.

PATROCLUS Your answer, sir.

THERSITES Fare ye well, with all my heart.

ACHILLES Why, but he is not in this tune, is he?

---

264 *jerkin* close-fitting jacket   **268** *put on* imitate

THERSITES No, but out of tune thus. What music will be
    in him when Hector has knocked out his brains, I know
    not ; but I am sure none, unless the fiddler Apollo get
    his sinews to make catlings on.   299

ACHILLES Come, thou shalt bear a letter to him straight.

THERSITES Let me bear another to his horse, for that's
    the more capable creature.   302

ACHILLES
    My mind is troubled, like a fountain stirred ;
    And I myself see not the bottom of it.
                        [Exeunt Achilles and Patroclus.]

THERSITES Would the fountain of your mind were clear
    again, that I might water an ass at it ! I had rather be a
    tick in a sheep than such a valiant ignorance.   [Exit.]

*

    Enter, at one door, Aeneas with a torch ; at another,   IV, i
    Paris, Deiphobus, Antenor, Diomed the Grecian,
    [and others,] with torches.

PARIS
    See, ho ! who is that there ?

DEIPHOBUS   It is the Lord Aeneas.

AENEAS
    Is the prince there in person ?
    Had I so good occasion to lie long
    As you, Prince Paris, nothing but heavenly business
    Should rob my bed-mate of my company.

DIOMEDES
    That's my mind too. Good morrow, Lord Aeneas.

PARIS
    A valiant Greek, Aeneas ; take his hand.
    Witness the process of your speech, wherein   8
    You told how Diomed, a whole week by days,   9

299 *catlings* strings of catgut   302 *capable* intelligent
IV, i Within the gates of Troy   8 *process* drift, gist   9 *by days* day by day

Did haunt you in the field.

AENEAS   Health to you, valiant sir,
11   During all question of the gentle truce ;
      But when I meet you armed, as black defiance
      As heart can think or courage execute.

DIOMEDES
      The one and other Diomed embraces.
      Our bloods are now in calm, and, so long, health !
16   But when contention and occasion meet,
      By Jove, I'll play the hunter for thy life
      With all my force, pursuit, and policy.

AENEAS
      And thou shalt hunt a lion that will fly
      With his face backward. In humane gentleness,
21   Welcome to Troy ! Now, by Anchises' life,
22   Welcome indeed ! By Venus' hand I swear,
      No man alive can love in such a sort
      The thing he means to kill more excellently.

DIOMEDES
      We sympathize. Jove, let Aeneas live,
      If to my sword his fate be not the glory,
      A thousand complete courses of the sun !
      But, in mine emulous honor, let him die
      With every joint a wound, and that to-morrow !

AENEAS
      We know each other well.

DIOMEDES
      We do, and long to know each other worse.

PARIS
      This is the most despiteful gentle greeting,
      The noblest hateful love, that e'er I heard of.
      What business, lord, so early ?

AENEAS
      I was sent for to the king ; but why, I know not.

11 *question . . . truce* conversation made possible by the truce   16 *occasion*
opportunity   21 *Anchises* Aeneas' father   22 *By Venus' hand* (Diomedes
had wounded Venus, mother of Aeneas, in the hand)

PARIS
    His purpose meets you ; 'twas to bring this Greek
    To Calchas' house, and there to render him,
    For the enfreed Antenor, the fair Cressid.
    Let's have your company ; or, if you please,
    Haste there before us. I constantly do think –   40
    Or rather call my thought a certain knowledge –
    My brother Troilus lodges there to-night.
    Rouse him and give him note of our approach,
    With the whole quality wherefore. I fear   44
    We shall be much unwelcome.

AENEAS   That I assure you.
    Troilus had rather Troy were borne to Greece
    Than Cressid borne from Troy.

PARIS   There is no help.
    The bitter disposition of the time
    Will have it so. On, lord ; we'll follow you.

AENEAS
    Good morrow, all.   *[Exit Aeneas.]*

PARIS
    And tell me, noble Diomed ; faith, tell me true,
    Even in the soul of sound good-fellowship,
    Who, in your thoughts, deserves fair Helen best,
    Myself or Menelaus ?

DIOMEDES   Both alike.
    He merits well to have her that doth seek her,
    Not making any scruple of her soilure,
    With such a hell of pain and world of charge ;   57
    And you as well to keep her that defend her,
    Not palating the taste of her dishonor,   59
    With such a costly loss of wealth and friends.
    He, like a puling cuckold, would drink up
    The lees and dregs of a flat tamèd piece ;   62

---

40 *constantly* firmly   44 *quality* explanation   57 *charge* cost   59 *Not palating* insensible of   62 *flat tamèd piece* cask so long opened that the wine is flat ; also piece of flesh

You, like a lecher, out of whorish loins
Are pleased to breed out your inheritors.
65   Both merits poised, each weighs nor less nor more;
But he as he, the heavier for a whore.

PARIS
You are too bitter to your countrywoman.

DIOMEDES
She's bitter to her country. Hear me, Paris:
For every false drop in her bawdy veins
70   A Grecian's life hath sunk; for every scruple
Of her contaminated carrion weight
A Troyan hath been slain. Since she could speak,
She hath not given so many good words breath
As for her Greeks and Troyans suff'red death.

PARIS
75   Fair Diomed, you do as chapmen do,
Dispraise the thing that you desire to buy;
But we in silence hold this virtue well,
We'll not commend what we intend to sell.
Here lies our way.   *Exeunt.*

*

IV, ii   *Enter Troilus and Cressida.*

TROILUS
Dear, trouble not yourself; the morn is cold.

CRESSIDA
Then, sweet my lord, I'll call mine uncle down;
He shall unbolt the gates.

TROILUS   Trouble him not;
4   To bed, to bed. Sleep kill those pretty eyes,
And give as soft attachment to thy senses
As infants' empty of all thought!

---

65 *poised* weighed **70** *scruple* the smallest unit of weight **75** *chapmen*
merchants
IV, ii The house of Pandarus **4** *kill* overpower

CRESSIDA   Good morrow then.
TROILUS
  I prithee now, to bed.
CRESSIDA   Are you aweary of me ?
TROILUS
  O Cressida, but that the busy day,
  Waked by the lark, hath roused the ribald crows,
  And dreaming night will hide our joys no longer,
  I would not from thee.
CRESSIDA   Night hath been too brief.
TROILUS
  Beshrew the witch ! with venomous wights she stays   12
  As tediously as hell, but flies the grasps of love
  With wings more momentary-swift than thought.
  You will catch cold and curse me.
CRESSIDA   Prithee, tarry ;
  You men will never tarry.
  O foolish Cressid ! I might have still held off,
  And then you would have tarried. Hark, there's one up.
PANDARUS *[within]* What's all the doors open here ?
TROILUS It is your uncle.
CRESSIDA A pestilence on him ! Now will he be mocking.
  I shall have such a life.
            Enter Pandarus.
PANDARUS How now, how now ! How go maidenheads ?
  Here, you maid, where's my cousin Cressid ?
CRESSIDA
  Go hang yourself, you naughty mocking uncle.
  You bring me to do – and then you flout me too.
PANDARUS To do what ? To do what ? Let her say what.
  What have I brought you to do ?
CRESSIDA
  Come, come ; beshrew your heart ! You'll ne'er be good,
  Nor suffer others.

12 *venomous* poisonous, i.e. doing evil

31 PANDARUS Ha, ha! Alas, poor wretch! A poor capocchia! Hast not slept to-night? Would he not, a naughty
man, let it sleep? A bugbear take him!

CRESSIDA
Did not I tell you? Would he were knocked i' th' head!
One knocks.
Who's that at door? Good uncle, go and see.
My lord, come you again into my chamber.
You smile and mock me, as if I meant naughtily.

TROILUS Ha, ha!

CRESSIDA
Come, you are deceived, I think of no such thing.
Knock.
How earnestly they knock! Pray you, come in.
I would not for half Troy have you seen here.
Exeunt [Troilus and Cressida].

PANDARUS Who's there? What's the matter? Will you
beat down the door? How now, what's the matter?
[Enter Aeneas.]

AENEAS
Good morrow, lord, good morrow.

PANDARUS Who's there? My Lord Aeneas! By my troth,
I knew you not. What news with you so early?

AENEAS
Is not Prince Troilus here?

PANDARUS Here? What should he do here?

AENEAS
Come, he is here, my lord. Do not deny him.
50 It doth import him much to speak with me.

PANDARUS Is he here, say you? 'Tis more than I know,
I'll be sworn. For my own part, I came in late. What
should he do here?

AENEAS Who! nay, then. Come, come, you'll do him
wrong ere you are ware. You'll be so true to him, to be

---

31 *capocchia* simpleton   50 *doth import* is important to

false to him. Do not you know of him, but yet go fetch
him hither ; go.
    [Enter Troilus.]

TROILUS How now, what's the matter ?

AENEAS
  My lord, I scarce have leisure to salute you,
  My matter is so rash. There is at hand   60
  Paris your brother, and Deiphobus,
  The Grecian Diomed, and our Antenor
  Delivered to us ; and for him forthwith,
  Ere the first sacrifice, within this hour,
  We must give up to Diomedes' hand
  The Lady Cressida.

TROILUS   Is it concluded so ?

AENEAS
  By Priam, and the general state of Troy.
  They are at hand and ready to effect it.

TROILUS
  How my achievements mock me !
  I will go meet them. And, my Lord Aeneas,   70
  We met by chance ; you did not find me here.

AENEAS
  Good, good, my lord ; the secrets of nature
  Have not more gift in taciturnity.

                  Exeunt [Troilus and Aeneas].

PANDARUS Is't possible ? No sooner got but lost ? The
devil take Antenor ! The young prince will go mad. A
plague upon Antenor ! I would they had broke 's neck !
    Enter Cressida.

CRESSIDA
  How now ? What's the matter ? Who was here ?

PANDARUS Ah, ah !

CRESSIDA
  Why sigh you so profoundly ? Where's my lord ?
  Gone ? Tell me, sweet uncle, what's the matter ?   80

60 *rash* urgent

PANDARUS Would I were as deep under the earth as I am
    above!

CRESSIDA O the gods! what's the matter?

PANDARUS Pray thee, get thee in. Would thou hadst
    ne'er been born! I knew thou wouldst be his death. O
    poor gentleman! A plague upon Antenor!

CRESSIDA Good uncle, I beseech you on my knees,
    what's the matter?

PANDARUS Thou must be gone, wench, thou must be
    gone; thou art changed for Antenor. Thou must to thy
    father and be gone from Troilus. 'Twill be his death;
92 'twill be his bane; he cannot bear it.

CRESSIDA

O you immortal gods! I will not go.

PANDARUS Thou must.

CRESSIDA

I will not, uncle. I have forgot my father;
I know no touch of consanguinity –
No kin, no love, no blood, no soul so near me
As the sweet Troilus. O you gods divine,
Make Cressid's name the very crown of falsehood
If ever she leave Troilus! Time, force, and death,
Do to this body what extremes you can;
But the strong base and building of my love
Is as the very centre of the earth,
Drawing all things to it. I'll go in and weep.

PANDARUS Do, do.

CRESSIDA

Tear my bright hair, and scratch my praisèd cheeks,
Crack my clear voice with sobs, and break my heart
With sounding Troilus. I will not go from Troy.

[Exeunt.]

*

92 *bane* destruction

Enter Paris, Troilus, Aeneas, Deiphobus, Antenor,   IV, iii
Diomedes.

PARIS

It is great morning, and the hour prefixed   1
For her delivery to this valiant Greek
Comes fast upon. Good my brother Troilus,
Tell you the lady what she is to do,
And haste her to the purpose.

TROILUS   Walk into her house.
I'll bring her to the Grecian presently;   6
And to his hand when I deliver her,
Think it an altar, and thy brother Troilus
A priest there off'ring to it his own heart.

PARIS

I know what 'tis to love;
And would as I shall pity, I could help!
Please you walk in, my lords.   *Exeunt.*

*

Enter Pandarus and Cressida.   IV, iv

PANDARUS Be moderate, be moderate.

CRESSIDA

Why tell you me of moderation?
The grief is fine, full, perfect, that I taste,
And violenteth in a sense as strong   4
As that which causeth it. How can I moderate it?
If I could temporize with my affections,
Or brew it to a weak and colder palate,   7
The like allayment could I give my grief.
My love admits no qualifying dross;
No more my grief, in such a precious loss.
     Enter Troilus.

PANDARUS Here, here, here he comes. Ah, sweet ducks!

IV, iii Outside the house of Pandarus   1 *great morning* broad daylight
6 *presently* at once
IV, iv The house of Pandarus   4 *violenteth* rages   7 *palate* taste

CRESSIDA [*embracing him*] O Troilus! Troilus!

13 PANDARUS What a pair of spectacles is here! Let me embrace too. 'O heart,' as the goodly saying is –

> O heart, heavy heart,
> Why sigh'st thou without breaking?

where he answers again,

> Because thou canst not ease thy smart
> By friendship nor by speaking.

There was never a truer rhyme. Let us cast away nothing, for we may live to have need of such a verse. We see it, we see it. How now, lambs!

TROILUS
23 Cressid, I love thee in so strained a purity,
24 That the blest gods, as angry with my fancy,
More bright in zeal than the devotion which
Cold lips blow to their deities, take thee from me.

CRESSIDA Have the gods envy?

PANDARUS Ay, ay, ay, ay; 'tis too plain a case.

CRESSIDA
And is it true that I must go from Troy?

TROILUS
A hateful truth.

CRESSIDA   What, and from Troilus too?

TROILUS
From Troy and Troilus.

CRESSIDA   Is't possible?

TROILUS
32 And suddenly, where injury of chance
Puts back leave-taking, justles roughly by
All time of pause, rudely beguiles our lips
35 Of all rejoindure, forcibly prevents
Our locked embrasures, strangles our dear vows
Even in the birth of our own laboring breath.
We two, that with so many thousand sighs
Did buy each other, must poorly sell ourselves

---

13 *spectacles* (a pun) 23 *strained* filtered, purified 24 *fancy* love 32
injury of chance injurious accident 35 *rejoindure* joining again

With the rude brevity and discharge of one.
Injurious time now with a robber's haste
Crams his rich thiev'ry up, he knows not how.
As many farewells as be stars in heaven,
With distinct breath and consigned kisses to them,   44
He fumbles up into a loose adieu,   45
And scants us with a single famished kiss,
Distasted with the salt of broken tears.   47

AENEAS *(within)* My lord, is the lady ready?

TROILUS
Hark! you are called. Some say the Genius   49
Cries so to him that instantly must die.
Bid them have patience; she shall come anon.

PANDARUS Where are my tears? Rain, to lay this wind,
or my heart will be blown up by the root!   *[Exit.]*

CRESSIDA
I must, then, to the Grecians?

TROILUS   No remedy.

CRESSIDA
A woeful Cressid 'mongst the merry Greeks!
When shall we see again?

TROILUS
Hear me, love. Be thou but true of heart –

CRESSIDA
I true! How now! What wicked deem is this?   58

TROILUS
Nay, we must use expostulation kindly,
For it is parting from us.   60
I speak not 'be thou true' as fearing thee,
For I will throw my glove to Death himself   62
That there's no maculation in thy heart;   63
But 'be thou true,' say I, to fashion in   64

44 *With . . . them* with the words of farewell and kisses that should ratify
each 45 *fumbles* wraps up clumsily 47 *Distasted* tasting bad 49 *Genius*
a man's attendant spirit 58 *deem* thought 60 *it . . . us* we are saying good-
bye 62 *throw my glove* give a challenge 63 *maculation* taint of disloyalty
64–65 *fashion . . . protestation* furnish a pattern for my own promise that
follows

My sequent protestation; be thou true,
And I will see thee.

CRESSIDA

O, you shall be exposed, my lord, to dangers
As infinite as imminent; but I'll be true.

TROILUS

And I'll grow friend with danger. Wear this sleeve.

CRESSIDA

And you this glove. When shall I see you?

TROILUS

I will corrupt the Grecian sentinels,
To give thee nightly visitation.
But yet, be true.

CRESSIDA   O heavens! 'be true' again!

TROILUS

Hear why I speak it, love.
75 The Grecian youths are full of quality;
[They're loving, well composed, with gift of nature,]
77 And swelling o'er with arts and exercise.
78 How novelty may move, and parts with person,
Alas! a kind of godly jealousy –
Which, I beseech you, call a virtuous sin –
Makes me afeared.

CRESSIDA   O heavens, you love me not!

TROILUS

Die I a villain, then!
In this I do not call your faith in question
So mainly as my merit. I cannot sing,
85 Nor heel the high lavolt, nor sweeten talk,
Nor play at subtle games – fair virtues all,
87 To which the Grecians are most prompt and pregnant;
But I can tell that in each grace of these
89 There lurks a still and dumb-discoursive devil

---

75 *quality* good qualities 77 *arts and exercise* i.e. theory and practice
78 *parts with person* accomplishments with personal charm 85 *lavolt*
a lively dance 87 *pregnant* ready 89 *dumb-discoursive* speakingly in
silence

That tempts most cunningly. But be not tempted.
CRESSIDA Do you think I will?
TROILUS No.
But something may be done that we will not;
And sometimes we are devils to ourselves
When we will tempt the frailty of our powers,
Presuming on their changeful potency.   96
AENEAS *(within)*
Nay, good my lord!
TROILUS   Come, kiss; and let us part.
PARIS *(within)*
Brother Troilus!
TROILUS   Good brother, come you hither;
And bring Aeneas and the Grecian with you.
CRESSIDA
My lord, will you be true?
TROILUS
Who? I? Alas, it is my vice, my fault.
Whiles others fish with craft for great opinion,   102
I with great truth catch mere simplicity;
Whilst some with cunning gild their copper crowns,
With truth and plainess I do wear mine bare.
Fear not my truth; the moral of my wit   106
Is 'plain and true'; there's all the reach of it.
        [*Enter Aeneas, Paris, Antenor, Deiphobus, and
        Diomedes.*]
Welcome, Sir Diomed. Here is the lady
Which for Antenor we deliver you.
At the port, lord, I'll give her to thy hand,   110
And by the way possess thee what she is.   111
Entreat her fair; and, by my soul, fair Greek,   112
If e'er thou stand at mercy of my sword,
Name Cressid, and thy life shall be as safe
As Priam is in Ilion.

96 *changeful potency* power that may change (to failure)   102 *opinion*
reputation for wisdom   106 *moral* maxim   110 *port* gate   111 *possess*
make known to   112 *Entreat* treat

DIOMEDES   Fair Lady Cressid,
So please you, save the thanks this prince expects.
The lustre in your eye, heaven in your cheek,
Pleads your fair usage ; and to Diomed
You shall be mistress, and command him wholly.

TROILUS
Grecian, thou dost not use me courteously,
121 To shame the seal of my petition to thee
In praising her. I tell thee, lord of Greece,
She is as far high-soaring o'er thy praises
As thou unworthy to be called her servant.
125 I charge thee use her well, even for my charge ;
For, by the dreadful Pluto, if thou dost not,
Though the great bulk Achilles be thy guard,
I'll cut thy throat.

DIOMEDES   O, be not moved, Prince Troilus.
Let me be privileged by my place and message
To be a speaker free. When I am hence,
131 I'll answer to my lust ; and know you, lord,
I'll nothing do on charge. To her own worth
She shall be prized ; but that you say 'be't so,'
I'll speak it in my spirit and honor, 'no.'

TROILUS
Come, to the port. I'll tell thee, Diomed,
136 This brave shall oft make thee to hide thy head.
Lady, give me your hand, and, as we walk,
To our own selves bend we our needful talk.
                    [Exeunt Troilus, Cressida, and Diomedes.]
               Sound trumpet.

PARIS
Hark ! Hector's trumpet.

AENEAS   How have we spent this morning !
The prince must think me tardy and remiss,
That swore to ride before him to the field.

121 *shame the seal of* treat disdainfully my promise given in exchange for
125 *even for my charge* merely because I tell you to   131 *answer . . . lust* do as
I please   136 *brave* boast

PARIS
  'Tis Troilus' fault. Come, come, to field with him.
[DEIPHOBUS
  Let us make ready straight.
AENEAS
  Yea, with a bridegroom's fresh alacrity,
  Let us address to tend on Hector's heels.
  The glory of our Troy doth this day lie
  On his fair worth and single chivalry.]   *Exeunt.*

*

Enter Ajax, armed ; Achilles, Patroclus, Agamem-   IV, v
non, Menelaus, Ulysses, Nestor, Calchas, &c.

AGAMEMNON
  Here art thou in appointment fresh and fair,   1
  Anticipating time. With starting courage,   2
  Give with thy trumpet a loud note to Troy,
  Thou dreadful Ajax, that the appallèd air
  May pierce the head of the great combatant
  And hale him hither.
AJAX   Thou, trumpet, there's my purse.   6
  Now crack thy lungs, and split thy brazen pipe.
  Blow, villain, till thy spherèd bias cheek   8
  Outswell the colic of puffed Aquilon.   9
  Come, stretch thy chest, and let thy eyes spout blood ;
  Thou blowest for Hector.
      [*Trumpet sounds.*]
ULYSSES
  No trumpet answers.
ACHILLES   'Tis but early days.   12
AGAMEMNON
  Is not yond Diomed with Calchas' daughter ?

IV, v The Grecian camp   1 *appointment* equipment   2 *starting* active
6 *trumpet* trumpeter   8 *bias* puffed-out   9 *colic . . . Aquilon* the north
wind, personified, distended by colic   12 *days* in the day

ULYSSES
'Tis he, I ken the manner of his gait ;
He rises on the toe. That spirit of his
In aspiration lifts him from the earth.
[Enter Diomedes, with Cressida.]

AGAMEMNON
Is this the Lady Cressid ?

DIOMEDES   Even she.

AGAMEMNON
Most dearly welcome to the Greeks, sweet lady.

NESTOR
Our general doth salute you with a kiss.

ULYSSES
20   Yet is the kindness but particular.
21   'Twere better she were kissed in general.

NESTOR
And very courtly counsel. I'll begin.
So much for Nestor.

ACHILLES
I'll take that winter from your lips, fair lady.
Achilles bids you welcome.

MENELAUS
I had good argument for kissing once.

PATROCLUS
But that's no argument for kissing now ;
28   For thus popped Paris in his hardiment,
29   And parted thus you and your argument.

ULYSSES
O, deadly gall, and theme of all our scorns !
For which we lose our heads to gild his horns.

PATROCLUS
The first was Menelaus' kiss ; this, mine :
Patroclus kisses you.

MENELAUS   O, this is trim.

20 *particular* single   **21** *in general* (1) by the general, (2) universally   **28**
hardiment boldness   **29** *argument* i.e. Helen

114

PATROCLUS
  Paris and I kiss evermore for him.
MENELAUS
  I'll have my kiss, sir. Lady, by your leave.
CRESSIDA
  In kissing, do you render or receive ?
PATROCLUS
  Both take and give.
CRESSIDA   I'll make my match to live,   37
  The kiss you take is better than you give ;
  Therefore no kiss.
MENELAUS
  I'll give you boot ; I'll give you three for one.   40
CRESSIDA
  You are an odd man ; give even, or give none.   41
MENELAUS
  An odd man, lady ? Every man is odd.
CRESSIDA
  No, Paris is not, for you know 'tis true
  That you are odd and he is even with you.
MENELAUS
  You fillip me o' th' head.   45
CRESSIDA   No, I'll be sworn.
ULYSSES
  It were no match, your nail against his horn.   46
  May I, sweet lady, beg a kiss of you ?
CRESSIDA
  You may.
ULYSSES   I do desire it.
CRESSIDA   Why, beg then.
ULYSSES
  Why, then, for Venus' sake, give me a kiss,
  When Helen is a maid again, and his –

---

37 *make . . . live* wager my life   40 *boot* odds   41 *odd* i.e. singular and
single   45 *fillip* tap   46 *It . . . horn* your nail, in tapping, would be no
match for his hard horn

CRESSIDA
I am your debtor; claim it when 'tis due.

ULYSSES
Never's my day, and then a kiss of you.

DIOMEDES
Lady, a word. I'll bring you to your father.
                    [*Exeunt Diomedes and Cressida.*]

NESTOR
A woman of quick sense.

ULYSSES   Fie, fie upon her!
There's language in her eye, her cheek, her lip;
Nay, her foot speaks. Her wanton spirits look out
57   At every joint and motive of her body.
O, these encounterers, so glib of tongue,
59   That give a coasting welcome ere it comes,
60   And wide unclasp the tables of their thoughts
To every ticklish reader, set them down
62   For sluttish spoils of opportunity
And daughters of the game.
          Flourish. Enter all of Troy [*Hector, Paris, Aeneas,*
          Helenus, Troilus, and Attendants].

ALL
The Troyans' trumpet.

AGAMEMNON   Yonder comes the troop.

AENEAS
Hail, all the state of Greece. What shall be done
To him that victory commands? Or do you purpose
A victor shall be known? Will you the knights
Shall to the edge of all extremity
Pursue each other, or shall they be divided
By any voice or order of the field?
Hector bade ask.

AGAMEMNON   Which way would Hector have it?

AENEAS
He cares not; he'll obey conditions.

57 *motive* moving part   59 *coasting* sidelong   60 *tables* tablets   62–63
For . . . game for harlots who yield at every opportunity

ACHILLES
  'Tis done like Hector ; but securely done,   73
  A little proudly, and great deal misprising
  The knight opposed.
AENEAS   If not Achilles, sir,
  What is your name ?
ACHILLES   If not Achilles, nothing.
AENEAS
  Therefore Achilles ; but, whate'er, know this :
  In the extremity of great and little,
  Valor and pride excel themselves in Hector :
  The one almost as infinite as all,
  The other blank as nothing. Weigh him well,
  And that which looks like pride is courtesy.
  This Ajax is half made of Hector's blood,   83
  In love whereof half Hector stays at home ;
  Half heart, half hand, half Hector comes to seek
  This blended knight, half Troyan, and half Greek.
ACHILLES
  A maiden battle, then ? O, I perceive you.   87
      [Enter Diomedes.]
AGAMEMNON
  Here is Sir Diomed. Go, gentle knight,
  Stand by our Ajax. As you and Lord Aeneas
  Consent upon the order of their fight,   90
  So be it ; either to the uttermost,
  Or else a breath. The combatants being kin   92
  Half stints their strife before their strokes begin.
      [Ajax and Hector enter the lists.]
[ULYSSES
  They are opposed already.]
AGAMEMNON
  What Troyan is that same that looks so heavy ?   95

73 *securely* over-confidently   83 *Hector's blood* (cf. II, ii, 77)   87 *maiden*
bloodless, like that of men in training   90 *Consent* agree   92 *a breath*
merely exercise   95 *heavy* heavy-hearted

ULYSSES
The youngest son of Priam, a true knight,
Not yet mature, yet matchless, firm of word,
98 Speaking in deeds and deedless in his tongue,
Not soon provoked, nor being provoked soon calmed;
100 His heart and hand both open and both free,
For what he has he gives, what thinks he shows;
Yet gives he not till judgment guide his bounty,
103 Nor dignifies an impare thought with breath;
Manly as Hector, but more dangerous;
105 For Hector, in his blaze of wrath, subscribes
To tender objects, but he in heat of action
Is more vindicative than jealous love.
They call him Troilus, and on him erect
A second hope as fairly built as Hector.
Thus says Aeneas, one that knows the youth
111 Even to his inches, and with private soul
Did in great Ilion thus translate him to me.
Alarum. [Hector and Ajax fight.]

AGAMEMNON
They are in action.

NESTOR
Now, Ajax, hold thine own!

TROILUS   Hector, thou sleep'st; awake thee!

AGAMEMNON
His blows are well disposed. There, Ajax!

DIOMEDES
You must no more.
         Trumpets cease.

AENEAS   Princes, enough, so please you.

AJAX
I am not warm yet; let us fight again.

---

98 *deedless . . . tongue* not boastful **100** *free* open, generous **103** *impare* unequal to his judgment **105-06** *subscribes . . . objects* grants terms to the defenseless **111** *Even to his inches* from top to toe; *with private soul* in confidence

DIOMEDES
    As Hector pleases.
HECTOR   Why, then will I no more.
    Thou art, great lord, my father's sister's son,
    A cousin-german to great Priam's seed;
    The obligation of our blood forbids
    A gory emulation 'twixt us twain.
    Were thy commixtion Greek and Troyan so   123
    That thou couldst say, 'This hand is Grecian all,
    And this is Troyan; the sinews of this leg
    All Greek, and this all Troy; my mother's blood
    Runs on the dexter cheek, and this sinister   127
    Bounds in my father's,' by Jove multipotent,   128
    Thou shouldst not bear from me a Greekish member
    Wherein my sword had not impressure made
    [Of our rank feud.] But the just gods gainsay
    That any drop thou borrowedst from thy mother,
    My sacred aunt, should by my mortal sword
    Be drained! Let me embrace thee, Ajax;
    By him that thunders, thou hast lusty arms;   135
    Hector would have them fall upon him thus.   136
    Cousin, all honor to thee!
AJAX   I thank thee, Hector.
    Thou art too gentle and too free a man.
    I came to kill thee, cousin, and bear hence
    A great addition earnèd in thy death.
HECTOR
    Not Neoptolemus so mirable,   141
    On whose bright crest Fame with her loud'st 'Oyes'   142
    Cries, 'This is he!' could promise to himself
    A thought of added honor torn from Hector.
AENEAS
    There is expectance here from both the sides,

---

123 *commixtion* composition **127** *dexter, sinister* right, left **128** *multipotent* of many powers **135** *him that thunders* Zeus **136** *thus* in an embrace **141** *Neoptolemus* (cf. III. iii, 209n.; but perhaps Achilles is meant here); *mirable* wonderful **142** *Oyes* cry beginning a herald's proclamation

What further you will do.

HECTOR   We'll answer it;
147   The issue is embracement. Ajax, farewell.

AJAX

If I might in entreaties find success –
149   As seld I have the chance – I would desire
My famous cousin to our Grecian tents.

DIOMEDES

'Tis Agamemnon's wish, and great Achilles
Doth long to see unarmed the valiant Hector.

HECTOR

Aeneas, call my brother Troilus to me,
And signify this loving interview
155   To the expecters of our Troyan part.
156   Desire them home. Give me thy hand, my cousin;
I will go eat with thee and see your knights.
        [Agamemnon and the rest approach them.]

AJAX

Great Agamemnon comes to meet us here.

HECTOR

The worthiest of them tell me name by name;
But for Achilles, mine own searching eyes
Shall find him by his large and portly size.

AGAMEMNON

Worthy all arms *[embraces him]*, as welcome as to one
That would be rid of such an enemy –
[But that's no welcome. Understand more clear,
What's past and what's to come is strewed with husks
And formless ruin of oblivion;
167   But in this extant moment, faith and troth,
168   Strained purely from all hollow bias-drawing,
Bids thee, with most divine integrity,]
From heart of very heart, great Hector, welcome.

---

147 *issue* outcome   **149** *seld* seldom   **155** *expecters . . . part* Trojans waiting
for news   **156** *Desire them home* ask them to go home   **167** *extant* present
168 *bias-drawing* tortuous dealings (like the course given by the bias to the
bowl in bowling)

HECTOR
I thank thee, most imperious Agamemnon.

AGAMEMNON *[to Troilus]*
My well-famed lord of Troy, no less to you.

MENELAUS
Let me confirm my princely brother's greeting.
You brace of warlike brothers, welcome hither.

HECTOR
Who must we answer ?

AENEAS   The noble Menelaus.

HECTOR
O, you, my lord ? By Mars his gauntlet, thanks !
Mock not that I affect th' untraded oath ;   177
Your quondam wife swears still by Venus' glove.
She's well, but bade me not commend her to you.

MENELAUS
Name her not now, sir ; she's a deadly theme.

HECTOR
O, pardon ! I offend.

NESTOR
I have, thou gallant Troyan, seen thee oft,
Laboring for destiny, make cruel way   183
Through ranks of Greekish youth, and I have seen thee,
As hot as Perseus, spur thy Phrygian steed,
Despising many forfeits and subduements,   186
When thou hast hung thy advancèd sword i' th' air,   187
Not letting it decline on the declinèd,
That I have said to some my standers-by,
'Lo, Jupiter is yonder, dealing life !'   190
And I have seen thee pause and take thy breath,
When that a ring of Greeks have shraped thee in,   192
Like an Olympian wrestling. This have I seen ;

177 *untraded* unused   183 *Laboring for destiny* i.e. causing destined deaths
186 *Despising . . . subduements* ignoring the vanquished whose lives were
forfeit   187 *hung* held suspended   190 *dealing life* i.e. by not dealing death
192 *shraped* trapped

194 But this thy countenance, still locked in steel,
195 I never saw till now. I knew thy grandsire,
And once fought with him. He was a soldier good;
But, by great Mars, the captain of us all,
Never like thee. Let an old man embrace thee;
And, worthy warrior, welcome to our tents.

AENEAS
'Tis the old Nestor.

HECTOR
Let me embrace thee, good old chronicle,
That hast so long walked hand in hand with time.
Most reverend Nestor, I am glad to clasp thee.

NESTOR
I would my arms could match thee in contention,
[As they contend with thee in courtesy.]

HECTOR
I would they could.

NESTOR
Ha,
By this white beard, I'd fight with thee to-morrow.
Well, welcome, welcome. I have seen the time –

ULYSSES
I wonder now how yonder city stands,
When we have here her base and pillar by us.

HECTOR
212 I know your favor, Lord Ulysses, well.
Ah, sir, there's many a Greek and Troyan dead,
Since first I saw yourself and Diomed
In Ilion, on your Greekish embassy.

ULYSSES
Sir, I foretold you then what would ensue.
My prophecy is but half his journey yet,
For yonder walls, that pertly front your town,
Yon towers, whose wanton tops do buss the clouds,

---

194 *still* always   195 *grandsire* Laomedom, who built the walls of Troy
212 *favor* face

Must kiss their own feet.

HECTOR   I must not believe you.   220
There they stand yet, and modestly I think,
The fall of every Phrygian stone will cost
A drop of Grecian blood. The end crowns all,
And that old common arbitrator, Time,
Will one day end it.

ULYSSES   So to him we leave it.
Most gentle and most valiant Hector, welcome.
After the general, I beseech you next
To feast with me and see me at my tent.

ACHILLES
I shall forestall thee, Lord Ulysses, thou!
Now, Hector, I have fed mine eyes on thee;
I have with exact view perused thee, Hector,
And quoted joint by joint.   232

HECTOR   Is this Achilles?

ACHILLES
I am Achilles.

HECTOR
Stand fair, I prithee; let me look on thee.

ACHILLES
Behold thy fill.

HECTOR   Nay, I have done already.

ACHILLES
Thou art too brief. I will the second time,
As I would buy thee, view thee limb by limb.

HECTOR
O, like a book of sport thou'lt read me o'er;
But there's more in me than thou understand'st.
Why dost thou so oppress me with thine eye?

ACHILLES
Tell me, you heavens, in which part of his body
Shall I destroy him, whether there, or there, or there?

232 *quoted* marked

That I may give the local wound a name,
And make distinct the very breach whereout
Hector's great spirit flew. Answer me, heavens!

HECTOR
It would discredit the blessed gods, proud man,
To answer such a question. Stand again.
248 Think'st thou to catch my life so pleasantly
249 As to prenominate in nice conjecture
Where thou wilt hit me dead?

ACHILLES   I tell thee, yea.

HECTOR
Wert thou an oracle to tell me so,
I'd not believe thee. Henceforth guard thee well,
For I'll not kill thee there, nor there, nor there;
254 But, by the forge that stithied Mars his helm,
I'll kill thee everywhere, yea, o'er and o'er.
You wisest Grecians, pardon me this brag.
His insolence draws folly from my lips;
But I'll endeavor deeds to match these words,
Or may I never –

AJAX   Do not chafe thee, cousin;
And you, Achilles, let these threats alone,
Till accident or purpose bring you to't.
You may have every day enough of Hector,
263 If you have stomach. The general state, I fear,
Can scarce entreat you to be odd with him.

HECTOR
I pray you, let us see you in the field.
266 We have had pelting wars since you refused
The Grecians' cause.

ACHILLES   Dost thou entreat me, Hector?
268 To-morrow do I meet thee, fell as death;

248 *pleasantly* merrily   249 *prenominate* name beforehand; *nice* precise
254 *stithied* forged   263 *stomach* inclination   263–64 *The general . . . him*
i.e. you will have to do it on private impulse, since you will not do it when
the Greek leaders ask you   266 *pelting* petty   268 *fell* fierce

To-night all friends.

HECTOR   Thy hand upon that match.

AGAMEMNON

First, all you peers of Greece, go to my tent;
There in the full convive we. Afterwards,   271
As Hector's leisure and your bounties shall
Concur together, severally entreat him   273
To taste your bounties. Let the trumpets blow,
That this great soldier may his welcome know.

           Exeunt [all except Troilus and Ulysses].

TROILUS

My Lord Ulysses, tell me, I beseech you,
In what place of the field doth Calchas keep?   277

ULYSSES

At Menelaus' tent, most princely Troilus.
There Diomed doth feast with him to-night;
Who neither looks upon the heaven nor earth,
But gives all gaze and bent of amorous view
On the fair Cressid.

TROILUS

Shall I, sweet lord, be bound to thee so much,
After we part from Agamemnon's tent,
To bring me thither?

ULYSSES   You shall command me, sir.
As gentle tell me, of what honor was
This Cressida in Troy? Had she no lover there
That wails her absence?

TROILUS

O, sir, to such as boasting show their scars
A mock is due. Will you walk on, my lord?
She was beloved, she loved; she is, and doth:
But still sweet love is food for fortune's tooth.   *Exeunt*.

*

271 *convive* feast   273 *severally entreat* individually invite   277 *keep* dwell

V, i   *Enter Achilles and Patroclus.*

ACHILLES
I'll heat his blood with Greekish wine to-night,
Which with my scimitar I'll cool to-morrow.
Patroclus, let us feast him to the height.

PATROCLUS
Here comes Thersites.
        Enter Thersites.

ACHILLES   How now, thou cur of envy!
5   Thou crusty batch of nature, what's the news?

THERSITES Why, thou picture of what thou seemest, and
idol of idiot-worshippers, here's a letter for thee.

ACHILLES From whence, fragment?

THERSITES Why, thou full dish of fool, from Troy.

10 PATROCLUS Who keeps the tent now?

11 THERSITES The surgeon's box or the patient's wound.

PATROCLUS Well said, adversity, and what need these
tricks?

THERSITES Prithee, be silent, boy; I profit not by thy
talk. Thou art said to be Achilles' male varlet.

PATROCLUS Male varlet, you rogue! What's that?

THERSITES Why, his masculine whore. Now, the rotten
diseases of the south, the guts-griping ruptures, catarrhs,
18 loads o' gravel in the back, lethargies, cold palsies, raw
eyes, dirt-rotten livers, wheezing lungs, bladders full of
20 imposthume, sciaticas, lime-kilns i' th' palm, incurable
21 bone-ache, and the rivelled fee-simple of the tetter, and
the like, take and take again such preposterous discoveries!

PATROCLUS Why, thou damnable box of envy, thou,
what means thou to curse thus?

V, i Before the tent of Achilles 5 *batch* bread of the same baking 10
Who . . . now (Thersites can no longer taunt Achilles for keeping to his tent)
11 *surgeon's box . . . wound* (play on *tent* in the sense of a lancet for probing
a wound) 18 *back* kidney; *lethargies* apoplexies; *cold palsies* paralysis
20 *imposthume* abscess; *lime-kilns* burnings 21 *rivelled* wrinkled; *tetter*
possibly chronic ringworm

THERSITES Do I curse thee?

PATROCLUS Why, no, you ruinous butt, you whoreson 27
indistinguishable cur, no. 28

THERSITES No? Why art thou then exasperate, thou idle
immaterial skein of sleave silk, thou green sarcenet flap 30
for a sore eye, thou tassel of a prodigal's purse, thou?
Ah, how the poor world is pestered with such water-
flies, diminutives of nature.

PATROCLUS Out, gall!

THERSITES Finch egg!

ACHILLES
My sweet Patroclus, I am thwarted quite
From my great purpose in to-morrow's battle.
Here is a letter from Queen Hecuba,
A token from her daughter, my fair love,
Both taxing me and gaging me to keep 40
An oath that I have sworn. I will not break it.
Fall Greeks, fail fame, honor or go or stay,
My major vow lies here; this I'll obey.
Come, come, Thersites, help to trim my tent;
This night in banqueting must all be spent.
Away, Patroclus!   *Exit [with Patroclus].*

THERSITES With too much blood and too little brain,
these two may run mad; but if with too much brain and
too little blood they do, I'll be a curer of madmen. Here's
Agamemnon, an honest fellow enough, and one that
loves quails, but he has not so much brain as ear-wax; and 51
the goodly transformation of Jupiter there, his brother, 52
the bull, the primitive statue and oblique memorial of 53
cuckolds; a thrifty shoeing-horn in a chain, hanging at 54
his brother's leg, to what form but that he is should wit

---

27 *ruinous butt* dilapidated cask   28 *indistinguishable* shapeless   30 *sleave silk* silk floss; *sarcenet* silk   40 *taxing* censuring; *gaging* binding to a promise   51 *quails* loose women   52 *Jupiter* (who changed himself into a bull to seduce Europa)   53 *primitive . . . memorial* i.e. having horns, the symbol of a cuckold   54 *thrifty* stingy   54 *hanging . . . leg* (so that he cannot be shaken off)

56 larded with malice and malice forced with wit turn him
    to? To an ass, were nothing; he is both ass and ox: to an
    ox, were nothing; he is both ox and ass. To be a dog, a
59 mule, a cat, a fitchew, a toad, a lizard, an owl, a puttock,
    or a herring without a roe, I would not care; but to be
    Menelaus! I would conspire against destiny. Ask me not
62 what I would be, if I were not Thersites, for I care not to
63 be the louse of a lazar, so I were not Menelaus. Hey-day,
    spirits and fires!
         Enter Agamemnon, Ulysses, Nestor, [Hector, Ajax,
         Troilus, Menelaus,] and Diomedes, with lights.

AGAMEMNON
    We go wrong, we go wrong.
AJAX   No, yonder 'tis;
    There, where we see the lights.
HECTOR   I trouble you.
AJAX
    No, not a whit.
ULYSSES   Here comes himself to guide you.
         [Enter Achilles.]
ACHILLES
    Welcome, brave Hector; welcome, princes all.
AGAMEMNON
    So now, fair prince of Troy, I bid good night.
    Ajax commands the guard to tend on you.
HECTOR
    Thanks and good night to the Greeks' general.
MENELAUS
    Good night, my lord.
HECTOR
    Good night, sweet Lord Menelaus.
74 THERSITES Sweet draught! 'Sweet,' quoth 'a! Sweet
    sink, sweet sewer.

---

56 *forced* stuffed   59 *fitchew* polecat; *puttock* kite (opprobrious, as feeding
on carrion)   62–63 *I care not to be* I wouldn't mind being   63 *lazar* leper
74 *draught* privy

ACHILLES
Good night and welcome both at once, to those
That go or tarry.
AGAMEMNON Good night.
Exeunt Agamemnon [and] Menelaus.
ACHILLES
Old Nestor tarries, and you too, Diomed,
Keep Hector company an hour or two.
DIOMEDES
I cannot, lord ; I have important business,
The tide whereof is now. Good night, great Hector.   82
HECTOR
Give me your hand.
ULYSSES *[aside to Troilus]* Follow his torch ; he goes
To Calchas' tent. I'll keep you company.
TROILUS
Sweet sir, you honor me.
HECTOR   And so, good night.
[Exeunt Diomedes, then Ulysses and Troilus.]
ACHILLES
Come, come, enter my tent.
Exeunt [Achilles, Hector, Ajax, and Nestor].
THERSITES That same Diomed's a false-hearted rogue, a
most unjust knave ; I will no more trust him when he
leers than I will a serpent when he hisses. He will spend
his mouth and promise like Brabbler the hound ; but
when he performs, astronomers foretell it, it is prodigi-
ous, there will come some change. The sun borrows of
the moon when Diomed keeps his word. I will rather
leave to see Hector than not to dog him. They say he   95
keeps a Troyan drab, and uses the traitor Calchas' tent.
I'll after – nothing but lechery ! All incontinent varlets !
Exit.

*

82 *tide* time   95 *leave to see* miss seeing

V, ii   *Enter Diomed.*

DIOMEDES What, are you up here, ho? Speak.

CALCHAS *[within]* Who calls?

DIOMEDES Diomed. Calchas, I think. Where's your daughter?

CALCHAS *[within]* She comes to you.

   Enter Troilus and Ulysses [; after them Thersites].

ULYSSES

Stand where the torch may not discover us.

   Enter Cressid.

TROILUS

Cressid comes forth to him.

DIOMEDES   How now, my charge!

CRESSIDA

Now, my sweet guardian! Hark, a word with you.
   [Whispers.]

TROILUS Yea, so familiar!

ULYSSES She will sing any man at first sight.

THERSITES And any man may sing her, if he can take her

11 cliff; she's noted.

DIOMEDES Will you remember?

CRESSIDA Remember? Yes.

DIOMEDES Nay, but do, then;

And let your mind be coupled with your words.

TROILUS What shall she remember?

ULYSSES List!

CRESSIDA

Sweet honey Greek, tempt me no more to folly.

THERSITES Roguery!

DIOMEDES

Nay, then —

20 CRESSIDA   I'll tell you what —

DIOMEDES

Foh, foh! come, tell a pin. You are forsworn.

V, ii Before the tent of Calchas   11 *cliff* musical clef; *noted* (pun on notes of music)

CRESSIDA
In faith, I cannot. What would you have me do ?
THERSITES A juggling trick – to be secretly open.
DIOMEDES
What did you swear you would bestow on me ?
CRESSIDA
I prithee, do not hold me to mine oath ;
Bid me do anything but that, sweet Greek.
DIOMEDES Good night.
TROILUS Hold, patience !
ULYSSES How now, Troyan ?
CRESSIDA Diomed –   30
DIOMEDES
No, no, good night ; I'll be your fool no more.
TROILUS
Thy better must.
CRESSIDA   Hark, a word in your ear.
TROILUS
O plague and madness !
ULYSSES
You are movèd, prince ; let us depart, I pray you,
Lest your displeasure should enlarge itself
To wrathful terms. This place is dangerous ;
The time right deadly. I beseech you, go.
TROILUS
Behold, I pray you !
ULYSSES   Nay, good my lord, go off ;
You flow to great distraction ; come, my lord.
TROILUS
I prithee, stay.
ULYSSES   You have not patience ; come.   40
TROILUS
I pray you, stay. By hell, and all hell's torments,
I will not speak a word !
DIOMEDES   And so, good night.
CRESSIDA
Nay, but you part in anger,

TROILUS   Doth that grieve thee?
O withered truth!
ULYSSES   How now, my lord!
TROILUS   By Jove,
I will be patient.
CRESSIDA   Guardian! Why, Greek!
DIOMEDES
Foh, foh! adieu; you palter.
CRESSIDA
In faith, I do not. Come hither once again.
ULYSSES
You shake, my lord, at something. Will you go?
You will break out.
TROILUS   She strokes his cheek!
ULYSSES   Come, come.
TROILUS
Nay, stay; by Jove, I will not speak a word.
There is between my will and all offenses
A guard of patience. Stay a little while.
53 THERSITES How the devil Luxury, with his fat rump and
54   potato finger, tickles these together. Fry, lechery, fry!
DIOMEDES But will you, then?
CRESSIDA
In faith, I will, la; never trust me else.
DIOMEDES
Give me some token for the surety of it.
CRESSIDA
I'll fetch you one.   *Exit*.
ULYSSES
You have sworn patience.
TROILUS   Fear me not, my lord;
I will not be myself, nor have cognition
Of what I feel. I am all patience.
          Enter Cressid.
THERSITES Now the pledge; now, now, now!

53 *Luxury* lechery   54 *potato* (considered to stimulate lechery)

132

CRESSIDA Here, Diomed, keep this sleeve.

TROILUS
O beauty, where is thy faith?

ULYSSES My lord –

[TROILUS
I will be patient; outwardly I will.]

CRESSIDA
You look upon that sleeve; behold it well.
He loved me – O false wench! Give't me again.

DIOMEDES
Whose was't?

CRESSIDA It is no matter, now I have't again.
I will not meet with you to-morrow night.
I prithee, Diomed, visit me no more.

THERSITES Now she sharpens. Well said, whetstone! 71

DIOMEDES
I shall have it. 72

CRESSIDA What, this?

DIOMEDES Ay, that.

CRESSIDA
O, all you gods! O pretty, pretty pledge!
Thy master now lies thinking in his bed
Of thee and me, and sighs, and takes my glove,
And gives memorial dainty kisses to it, 76
As I kiss thee. Nay, do not snatch it from me;
He that takes that doth take my heart withal.

DIOMEDES
I had your heart before; this follows it.

TROILUS
I did swear patience.

CRESSIDA
You shall not have it, Diomed; faith, you shall not;
I'll give you something else.

DIOMEDES
I will have this. Whose was it?

71 *sharpens* whets his desire   72 *shall* am determined to   76 *memorial* i o.
of remembrance

CRESSIDA   It is no matter.

DIOMEDES
Come, tell me whose it was.

CRESSIDA
'Twas one's that loved me better than you will.
But, now you have it, take it.

DIOMEDES   Whose was it?

CRESSIDA
87   By all Diana's waiting-women yond,
And by herself, I will not tell you whose.

DIOMEDES
To-morrow will I wear it on my helm,
And grieve his spirit that dares not challenge it.

TROILUS
Wert thou the devil, and wor'st it on thy horn,
It should be challenged.

CRESSIDA
Well, well, 'tis done, 'tis past. And yet it is not;
I will not keep my word.

DIOMEDES   Why then, farewell;
Thou never shalt mock Diomed again.

CRESSIDA
You shall not go. One cannot speak a word
97   But it straight starts you.

DIOMEDES   I do not like this fooling.

98   THERSITES Nor I, by Pluto; but that that likes not you
pleases me best.

DIOMEDES
What, shall I come? The hour?

CRESSIDA   Ay, come – O Jove! –
101   Do come – I shall be plagued.

DIOMEDES   Farewell till then.

CRESSIDA
Good night. I prithee, come.   [Exit Diomedes.]
Troilus, farewell. One eye yet looks on thee,

87 *Diana's waiting-women* stars attending the moon   97 *starts you* makes
you start off (angry)   98 *likes* pleases   101 *plagued* punished

134

But with my heart the other eye doth see.
Ah, poor our sex! this fault in us I find,   105
The error of our eye directs our mind.   106
What error leads must err. O, then conclude
Minds swayed by eyes are full of turpitude.   *Exit.*

THERSITES
A proof of strength she could not publish more,   109
Unless she say, 'My mind is now turned whore.'

ULYSSES
All's done, my lord.

TROILUS   It is.

ULYSSES   Why stay we, then?

TROILUS
To make a recordation to my soul
Of every syllable that here was spoke.
But if I tell how these two did co-act,
Shall I not lie in publishing a truth?
Sith yet there is a credence in my heart,
An esperance so obstinately strong,   117
That doth invert th' attest of eyes and ears,   118
As if those organs had deceptious functions,   119
Created only to calumniate.
Was Cressid here?

ULYSSES   I cannot conjure, Troyan.   121

TROILUS
She was not, sure.

ULYSSES   Most sure she was.

TROILUS
Why, **my** negation hath no taste of madness.

ULYSSES
Nor mine, my lord. Cressid was here but now.

TROILUS
Let it not be believed for womanhood!   125

105 *poor our sex* our poor sex   106 *error* wandering (both physical and
moral here)   109 *proof of strength* strong proof; *publish more* confess more
clearly   117 *esperance* hope   118 *attest* witness   119 *deceptious* deceiving
121 *conjure* raise spirits (instead of Cressida)   125 *for* for the sake of

Think we had mothers ; do not give advantage
To stubborn critics, apt, without a theme,
128   For depravation, to square the general sex
By Cressid's rule. Rather think this not Cressid.

ULYSSES
What hath she done, prince, that can soil our mothers ?

TROILUS
Nothing at all, unless that this were she.

132 THERSITES Will 'a swagger himself out on 's own eyes ?

TROILUS
This she ? No, this is Diomed's Cressida.
If beauty have a soul, this is not she ;
If souls guide vows, if vows be sanctimonies,
If sanctimony be the gods' delight,
137   If there be rule in unity itself,
138   This was not she. O madness of discourse,
That cause sets up with and against itself ;
140   Bi-fold authority, where reason can revolt
Without perdition, and loss assume all reason
Without revolt. This is, and is not, Cressid.
143   Within my soul there doth conduce a fight
144   Of this strange nature that a thing inseparate
Divides more wider than the sky and earth ;
And yet the spacious breadth of this division
Admits no orifice for a point as subtle
148   As Ariachne's broken woof to enter.
149   Instance, O instance, strong as Pluto's gates ;
Cressid is mine, tied with the bonds of heaven.
Instance, O instance, strong as heaven itself ;

128–29 *square . . . rule* measure all women by Cressida's standard (cf.
'carpenter's rule')   132 *swagger . . . eyes* (cf. 'walk out on his own eyes')
137 *If . . . itself* if it is a principle that Cressida must be one   138 *discourse*
reason   140–42 *where reason . . . revolt* where reason can revolt against
itself without self-destruction, and destruction can take control of reason
without its revolting   143 *conduce* go on   144 *thing inseparate* i.e. Cressida,
as herself indivisible   148 *Ariachne* properly Arachne (Minerva tore up her
fine-spun web in jealousy and turned her into a spider)   149 *Instance*
evidence, argument

The bonds of heaven are slipped, dissolved, and loosed;
And with another knot, five-finger-tied,
The fractions of her faith, orts of her love, 154
The fragments, scraps, the bits, and greasy relics
Of her o'er-eaten faith, are bound to Diomed. 156

ULYSSES
May worthy Troilus be half attachèd 157
With that which here his passion doth express?

TROILUS
Ay, Greek; and that shall be divulgèd well
In characters as red as Mars his heart
Inflamed with Venus. Never did young man fancy
With so eternal and so fixed a soul.
Hark, Greek: as much as I do Cressid love,
So much by weight hate I her Diomed;
That sleeve is mine that he'll bear on his helm;
Were it a casque composed by Vulcan's skill,
My sword should bite it. Not the dreadful spout
Which shipmen do the hurricano call,
Constringed in mass by the almighty sun, 169
Shall dizzy with more clamor Neptune's ear
In his descent than shall my prompted sword
Falling on Diomed.

THERSITES He'll tickle it for his concupy. 173

TROILUS
O Cressid! O false Cressid! false, false, false!
Let all untruths stand by thy stainèd name,
And they'll seem glorious.

ULYSSES   O, contain yourself;
Your passion draws ears hither.
          Enter Aeneas.

AENEAS
I have been seeking you this hour, my lord.

---

154 *orts* scraps (properly of food)   156 *o'er-eaten* i.e. she has swallowed
her word   157 *half attachèd* half as much affected (as his passion indicates)
169 *Constringed* drawn together   173 *it* i.e. Diomedes (contemptuous);
concupy concupiscence, lust

Hector, by this, is arming him in Troy;
Ajax, your guard, stays to conduct you home.

TROILUS

181   Have with you, prince. My courteous lord, adieu.
Farewell, revolted fair; and Diomed,
Stand fast, and wear a castle on thy head!

ULYSSES

I'll bring you to the gates.

TROILUS

Accept distracted thanks.

Exeunt Troilus, Aeneas, and Ulysses.

THERSITES Would I could meet that rogue Diomed. I
187   would croak like a raven; I would bode, I would bode.
Patroclus will give me anything for the intelligence of
this whore. The parrot will not do more for an almond
than he for a commodious drab. Lechery, lechery; still
wars and lechery; nothing else holds fashion. A burning
devil take them!   *Exit.*

*

V, iii   *Enter Hector and Andromache.*

ANDROMACHE

When was my lord so much ungently tempered,
To stop his ears against admonishment?
Unarm, unarm, and do not fight to-day.

HECTOR

4   You train me to offend you; get you in.
By all the everlasting gods, I'll go.

ANDROMACHE

6   My dreams will, sure, prove ominous to the day.

HECTOR

No more, I say.
Enter Cassandra.

181 *Have with you* come along   187 *bode* portend (like a raven, a bird of ill omen)
V, iii Before the palace of Priam   4 *train* tempt; *offend* injure   6 *ominous to the day* omens of the day's events

CASSANDRA   Where is my brother Hector?

ANDROMACHE

Here, sister; armed and bloody in intent.
Consort with me in loud and dear petition;
Pursue we him on knees, for I have dreamed
Of bloody turbulence, and this whole night
Hath nothing been but shapes and forms of slaughter.

CASSANDRA

O, 'tis true.

HECTOR   Ho, bid my trumpet sound.

CASSANDRA

No notes of sally, for the heavens, sweet brother.

HECTOR

Be gone, I say; the gods have heard me swear.

CASSANDRA

The gods are deaf to hot and peevish vows.   16
They are polluted off'rings, more abhorred
Than spotted livers in the sacrifice.

ANDROMACHE

O, be persuaded! Do not count it holy
[To hurt by being just. It is as lawful,
For we would give much, to use violent thefts,   21
And rob in the behalf of charity.

CASSANDRA]

It is the purpose that makes strong the vow;
But vows to every purpose must not hold.
Unarm, sweet Hector.

HECTOR   Hold you still, I say;
Mine honor keeps the weather of my fate.   26
Life every man holds dear; but the dear man   27
Holds honor far more precious-dear than life.

        Enter Troilus.

How now, young man; mean'st thou to fight to-day?

ANDROMACHE

Cassandra, call my father to persuade.   *Exit Cassandra.*

16 *peevish* perverse   21 *For* because   26 *keeps the weather* keeps to wind-
ward (the position of advantage)   27 *dear man* worthy man

HECTOR
No, faith, young Troilus; doff thy harness, youth;
I am to-day i' th' vein of chivalry.
Let grow thy sinews till their knots be strong,
34   And tempt not yet the brushes of the war.
Unarm thee, go, and doubt thou not, brave boy,
I'll stand to-day for thee and me and Troy.

TROILUS
Brother, you have a vice of mercy in you,
Which better fits a lion than a man.

HECTOR
What vice is that, good Troilus? Chide me for it.

TROILUS
When many times the captive Grecian falls,
Even in the fan and wind of your fair sword,
You bid them rise and live.

HECTOR
O, 'tis fair play.

TROILUS   Fool's play, by heaven, Hector.

HECTOR
How now, how now?

TROILUS   For th' love of all the gods,
Let's leave the hermit pity with our mother,
And when we have our armors buckled on,
The venomed vengeance ride upon our swords,
48   Spur them to ruthful work, rein them from ruth.

HECTOR
Fie, savage, fie!

49 **TROILUS**   Hector, then 'tis wars.

HECTOR
Troilus, I would not have you fight to-day.

TROILUS
Who should withhold me?
Not fate, obedience, nor the hand of Mars

---

34 *brushes* encounters   48 *ruthful* pitiful; *ruth* pity   49 *then 'tis wars* war is
like that

Beck'ning with fiery truncheon my retire;   53
Not Priamus and Hecuba on knees,
Their eyes o'ergallèd with recourse of tears;   55
Nor you, my brother, with your true sword drawn,
Opposed to hinder me, should stop my way,
[But by my ruin.]
    Enter Priam and Cassandra.

CASSANDRA
Lay hold upon him, Priam, hold him fast;
He is thy crutch. Now if thou lose thy stay,   60
Thou on him leaning, and all Troy on thee,
Fall all together.

PRIAM   Come, Hector, come; go back.
Thy wife hath dreamed, thy mother hath had visions,
Cassandra doth foresee, and I myself
Am like a prophet suddenly enrapt
To tell thee that this day is ominous:
Therefore, come back.

HECTOR   Aeneas is a-field;
And I do stand engaged to many Greeks,
Even in the faith of valor, to appear   69
This morning to them.

PRIAM   Ay, but thou shalt not go.

HECTOR
I must not break my faith.
You know me dutiful; therefore, dear sir,
Let me not shame respect, but give me leave   73
To take that course by your consent and voice,
Which you do here forbid me, royal Priam.

CASSANDRA
O Priam, yield not to him!

ANDROMACHE   Do not, dear father.

---

53 *truncheon* staff used to signal the end of a combat between two champions
55 *o'ergallèd* inflamed; *recourse* coursing down **60** *stay* prop **69** *faith of valor* word of honor of a brave man **73** *shame respect* disgrace the respect due a parent

HECTOR

Andromache, I am offended with you.

Upon the love you bear me, get you in.

Exit Andromache.

TROILUS

This foolish, dreaming, superstitious girl

80   Makes all these bodements.

CASSANDRA   O farewell, dear Hector!

Look, how thou diest; look, how thy eye turns pale;

Look, how thy wounds do bleed at many vents!

Hark, how Troy roars, how Hecuba cries out,

How poor Andromache shrills her dolors forth!

Behold, distraction, frenzy, and amazement,

86   Like witless antics, one another meet,

And all cry Hector! Hector's dead! O Hector!

TROILUS

Away! Away!

CASSANDRA

Farewell. Yet, soft: Hector, I take my leave.

Thou dost thyself and all our Troy deceive.   *[Exit.]*

HECTOR

You are amazed, my liege, at her exclaim.

Go in and cheer the town. We'll forth and fight;

Do deeds worth praise and tell you them at night.

PRIAM

Farewell. The gods with safety stand about thee.

[Exeunt Priam and Hector.] Alarum.

TROILUS

They are at it, hark. Proud Diomed, believe,

I come to lose my arm, or win my sleeve.

Enter Pandar.

PANDARUS Do you hear, my lord? Do you hear?

TROILUS What now?

PANDARUS Here's a letter come from yond poor girl.

TROILUS Let me read.

80 *bodements* ill omens   86 *antics* lunatics

142

PANDARUS A whoreson tisick, a whoreson rascally tisick 101
so troubles me, and the foolish fortune of this girl; and
what one thing, what another, that I shall leave you one
o' these days; and I have a rheum in mine eyes too, and
such an ache in my bones that, unless a man were
cursed, I cannot tell what to think on't. What says she
there?

TROILUS
Words, words, mere words, no matter from the heart;
Th' effect doth operate another way.
        [Tearing the letter.]
Go, wind to wind, there turn and change together.
My love with words and errors still she feeds,
But edifies another with her deeds.   Exeunt.

                        *

        [Alarum.] Excursions. Enter Thersites [in excursion]. V, iv
THERSITES Now they are clapper-clawing one another;
I'll go look on. That dissembling abominable varlet,
Diomed, has got that same scurvy doting foolish young
knave's sleeve of Troy there in his helm. I would fain
see them meet, that that same young Troyan ass, that
loves the whore there, might send that Greekish whore-
masterly villain with the sleeve back to the dissembling
luxurious drab, of a sleeveless errand. O' th' t' other 8
side, the policy of those crafty swearing rascals – that 9
stale old mouse-eaten dry cheese, Nestor, and that same
dog-fox, Ulysses – is not proved worth a blackberry.
They set me up, in policy, that mongrel cur, Ajax,
against that dog of as bad a kind, Achilles. And now is
the cur Ajax prouder than the cur Achilles, and will not
arm to-day. Whereupon the Grecians begin to proclaim 15
barbarism, and policy grows into an ill opinion.

101 *tisick* cough
V, iv Field before the walls of Troy   8 *sleeveless* fruitless   9 *crafty swearing*
i.e. crafty to the extent of perjury   15–16 *proclaim barbarism* set up the
authority of ignorance

[Enter Diomedes and Troilus.]
Soft! here comes sleeve, and t' other.

TROILUS
Fly not; for shouldst thou take the river Styx,
I would swim after.

DIOMEDES   Thou dost miscall retire.
20   I do not fly, but advantageous care
Withdrew me from the odds of multitude.
Have at thee!

23   THERSITES Hold thy whore, Grecian! Now for thy
whore, Troyan! Now the sleeve, now the sleeve!
                    [Exeunt Troilus and Diomedes, fighting.]
                    Enter Hector.

HECTOR
What art thou, Greek? Art thou for Hector's match?
Art thou of blood and honor?

THERSITES No, no. I am a rascal, a scurvy railing knave,
a very filthy rogue.

HECTOR
I do believe thee; live.   *[Exit.]*

THERSITES God-a-mercy, that thou wilt believe me; but
a plague break thy neck – for frighting me. What's become of the wenching rogues? I think they have swallowed one another. I would laugh at that miracle – yet,
in a sort, lechery eats itself. I'll seek them.   *Exit.*

V, v   *Enter Diomed and Servant.*

DIOMEDES
Go, go, my servant, take thou Troilus' horse;
Present the fair steed to my Lady Cressid.
Fellow, commend my service to her beauty;
Tell her I have chastised the amorous Troyan,
And am her knight by proof.

SERVANT   I go, my lord.   *[Exit.]*

20-21 *advantageous . . . multitude* care for my own advantage led me to
avoid facing heavy odds   23-24 *Hold . . . sleeve* (Thersites is urging both
men on impartially)

Enter Agamemnon.

AGAMEMNON

Renew, renew! The fierce Polydamas
Hath beat down Menon; bastard Margarelon
Hath Doreus prisoner,
And stands colossus-wise, waving his beam,   9
Upon the pashèd corses of the kings   10
Epistrophus and Cedius; Polixenes is slain,
Amphimachus and Thoas deadly hurt,
Patroclus ta'en or slain, and Palamedes
Sore hurt and bruisèd. The dreadful Sagittary   14
Appals our numbers. Haste we, Diomed,
To reinforcement, or we perish all.
       Enter Nestor.

NESTOR

Go, bear Patroclus' body to Achilles,
And bid the snail-paced Ajax arm for shame.
There is a thousand Hectors in the field.
Now here he fights on Galathe his horse,
And there lacks work; anon he's there afoot,
And there they fly or die, like scalèd sculls   22
Before the belching whale; then is he yonder,
And there the strawy Greeks, ripe for his edge,   24
Fall down before him, like a mower's swath.
Here, there, and everywhere, he leaves and takes,
Dexterity so obeying appetite
That what he will he does, and does so much
That proof is called impossibility.   29
       Enter Ulysses.

ULYSSES

O, courage, courage, princes! Great Achilles
Is arming, weeping, cursing, vowing vengeance.
Patroclus' wounds have roused his drowsy blood,

V, v   9 *beam* lance   10 *pashèd corses* battered corpses   14 *Sagittary* a
Centaur (half man, half horse) who aided the Trojans   22 *scalèd sculls*
scaly schools of fish   24 *strawy* i.e. like straw ripe for the mower's scythe
29 *proof* fact

Together with his mangled Myrmidons,
That noseless, handless, hacked and chipped, come to
 him,
Crying on Hector. Ajax hath lost a friend,
And foams at mouth, and he is armed and at it,
Roaring for Troilus, who hath done to-day
Mad and fantastic execution,
Engaging and redeeming of himself
With such a careless force and forceless care
As if that luck, in very spite of cunning,
Bade him win all.
   Enter Ajax.

AJAX
Troilus, thou coward Troilus!   *Exit.*
DIOMEDES   Ay, there, there.
NESTOR
So, so, we draw together.   *Exit.*
   Enter Achilles.
ACHILLES   Where is this Hector?
45   Come, come, thou boy-queller, show thy face;
Know what it is to meet Achilles angry.
Hector, where's Hector? I will none but Hector.   *Exit.*
V, vi   *Enter Ajax.*

AJAX
Troilus, thou coward Troilus, show thy head.
   Enter Diomedes.
DIOMEDES
Troilus, I say, where's Troilus?
AJAX   What wouldst thou?
DIOMEDES
I would correct him.
AJAX
Were I the general, thou shouldst have my office
5   Ere that correction. Troilus, I say; what, Troilus!
   Enter Troilus.

45 *boy-queller* boy-killer
V, vi   5 *correction* privilege of correcting Troilus

TROILUS
  O traitor Diomed! Turn thy false face, thou traitor,
  And pay thy life thou owest me for my horse.
DIOMEDES
  Ha, art thou there?
AJAX
  I'll fight with him alone. Stand, Diomed.
DIOMEDES
  He is my prize; I will not look upon.   10
TROILUS
  Come, both you cogging Greeks; have at you both!   11
                                [Exeunt, fighting.]
      [Enter Hector.]
HECTOR
  Yea, Troilus? O, well fought, my youngest brother!
      Enter Achilles.
ACHILLES
  Now do I see thee. Have at thee, Hector!
      [They fight.]
HECTOR
  Pause, if thou wilt.
ACHILLES
  I do disdain thy courtesy, proud Troyan.
  Be happy that my arms are out of use.
  My rest and negligence befriends thee now,
  But thou anon shalt hear of me again;
  Till when, go seek thy fortune.   *Exit.*
HECTOR   Fare thee well:
  I would have been much more a fresher man,
  Had I expected thee. How now, my brother!
      Enter Troilus.
TROILUS
  Ajax hath ta'en Aeneas! Shall it be?   22
  No, by the flame of yonder glorious heaven,
  He shall not carry him; I'll be ta'en too,

10 *look upon* remain a bystander 11 *cogging* deceitful 22 *ta'en* taken
captive

Or bring him off. Fate, hear me what I say!
I reck not though thou end my life to-day.   *Exit.*
    Enter one in armor.

HECTOR

Stand, stand, thou Greek; thou art a goodly mark.
No? Wilt thou not? I like thy armor well;
29 I'll frush it and unlock the rivets all,
But I'll be master of it. Wilt thou not, beast, abide?
Why then, fly on, I'll hunt thee for thy hide.
                                    Exit [in pursuit].

V, vii   *Enter Achilles with Myrmidons.*

ACHILLES

Come here about me, you my Myrmidons;
Mark what I say. Attend me where I wheel;
Strike not a stroke, but keep yourselves in breath;
And when I have the bloody Hector found,
5 Empale him with your weapons round about;
6 In fellest manner execute your arms.
Follow me, sirs, and my proceedings eye.
It is decreed, Hector the great must die.
                             Exit [with Myrmidons].
    *Enter Thersites, Menelaus, Paris [the last two
    fighting].*

THERSITES The cuckold and the cuckold-maker are at it.
10 Now, bull! now, dog! 'Loo, Paris, 'loo! Now, my
11 double-horned Spartan! 'Loo, Paris, 'loo! The bull has
the game; 'ware horns, ho! *Exeunt Paris and Menelaus.*
    Enter Bastard [Margarelon].

BASTARD Turn, slave, and fight.

THERSITES What art thou?

BASTARD A bastard son of Priam's.

THERSITES I am a bastard too; I love bastards. I am a
bastard begot, bastard instructed, bastard in mind,
bastard in valor, in everything illegitimate. One bear

---

29 *frush* batter
V, vii 5 *Empale him* fence him in 6 *execute* give effect to 10 *'Loo* (a
cry to excite dogs) 11–12 *has the game* wins

will not bite another, and wherefore should one bastard? Take heed, the quarrel 's most ominous to us. If
the son of a whore fight for a whore, he tempts judgment. Farewell, bastard.

BASTARD The devil take thee, coward!   *Exit.*
  Enter Hector.   V, viii

HECTOR
 Most putrefièd core, so fair without,
 Thy goodly armor thus hath cost thy life.
 Now is my day's work done; I'll take my breath.
 Rest, sword; thou hast thy fill of blood and death.
  [Puts off his helmet, and hangs his shield behind him.]
  Enter Achilles and his Myrmidons.

ACHILLES
 Look, Hector, how the sun begins to set,
 How ugly night comes breathing at his heels.
 Even with the vail and dark'ning of the sun,   7
 To close the day up, Hector's life is done.

HECTOR
 I am unarmed; forgo this vantage, Greek.

ACHILLES
 Strike, fellows, strike; this is the man I seek.
  [Hector falls.]
 So, Ilion, fall thou next! Come, Troy, sink down!
 Here lies thy heart, thy sinews, and thy bone.
 On, Myrmidons, and cry you all amain,
 'Achilles hath the mighty Hector slain!'
  Retreat.
 Hark, a retire upon our Grecian part.

GREEK
 The Troyan trumpets sound the like, my lord.

ACHILLES
 The dragon wing of night o'erspreads the earth,
 And, stickler-like, the armies separates.   18
 My half-supped sword, that frankly would have fed,   19

V, viii 7 *vail* going down 18 *stickler-like* like umpires parting combatants 19 *frankly* freely

Pleased with this dainty bait, thus goes to bed.
[Sheathes his sword.]
Come, tie his body to my horse's tail ;
Along the field I will the Troyan trail.   *Exeunt.*

V, ix   *Enter Agamemnon, Ajax, Menelaus, Nestor,*
          Diomed, and the rest, marching. [Sound retreat.
          Shout.]

AGAMEMNON
Hark, hark, what shout is that ?

NESTOR   Peace, drums !

SOLDIERS *(within)*   Achilles !
Achilles ! Hector 's slain ! Achilles !

DIOMEDES
3   The bruit is, Hector 's slain, and by Achilles.

AJAX
If it be so, yet bragless let it be ;
Great Hector was as good a man as he.

AGAMEMNON
March patiently along. Let one be sent
To pray Achilles see us at our tent.
If in his death the gods have us befriended,
Great Troy is ours, and our sharp wars are ended.

                              Exeunt.

V, x   *Enter Aeneas, Paris, Antenor, and Deiphobus.*

AENEAS
Stand, ho ! yet are we masters of the field.
Never go home ; here starve we out the night.
          Enter Troilus.

TROILUS
Hector is slain.

ALL   Hector ! The gods forbid !

TROILUS
He's dead and at the murderer's horse's tail,
In beastly sort, dragged through the shameful field.
Frown on, you heavens, effect your rage with speed ;

V, ix   3 *bruit* rumor

Sit, gods, upon your thrones, and smile at Troy.   7
I say, at once let your brief plagues be mercy,   8
And linger not our sure destructions on.

AENEAS

My lord, you do discomfort all the host.

TROILUS

You understand me not that tell me so.
I do not speak of flight, of fear, of death,
But dare all imminence that gods and men   13
Address their dangers in. Hector is gone.
Who shall tell Priam so, or Hecuba?
Let him that will a screech-owl aye be called
Go in to Troy, and say there Hector's dead.
There is a word will Priam turn to stone,
Make wells and Niobes of the maids and wives,   19
Cold statues of the youth, and in a word
Scare Troy out of itself. [But march away.
Hector is dead;] there is no more to say.
Stay yet. You vile abominable tents,
Thus proudly pight upon our Phrygian plains,   24
Let Titan rise as early as he dare,   25
I'll through and through you! And, thou great-sized   26
     coward,
No space of earth shall sunder our two hates.
I'll haunt thee like a wicked conscience still,
That mouldeth goblins swift as frenzy's thoughts.
Strike a free march to Troy. With comfort go;
Hope of revenge shall hide our inward woe.

     Enter Pandarus.

PANDARUS

But hear you, hear you!

V, x   7 *smile* i.e. in derision   8 *let . . . mercy* show mercy by letting your plagues destroy quickly   13–14 *But . . . dangers in* but dare whatever imminent dangers gods and men may be preparing   19 *Niobes* (Niobe, whose seven sons and seven daughters were slain, wept and was turned into a stone that still wept)   24 *pight* pitched   25 *Titan* (Helios, the sun, was one of the Titans)   26 *coward* i.e. Achilles

TROILUS

   Hence, broker lackey! Ignomy and shame
   Pursue thy life, and live aye with thy name.

                     Exeunt all but Pandarus.

PANDARUS A goodly medicine for my aching bones! O
   world, world! thus is the poor agent despised. O traitors
   and bawds, how earnestly are you set a-work, and
   how ill requited! Why should our endeavor be so
   loved, and the performance so loathed? What verse for
   it? What instance for it? Let me see.

      Full merrily the humble-bee doth sing,
      Till he hath lost his honey and his sting;
      And being once subdued in armèd tail,
      Sweet honey and sweet notes together fail.

45   Good traders in the flesh, set this in your painted cloths:
   'As many as be here of Pandar's hall,
   Your eyes, half out, weep out at Pandar's fall;
   Or if you cannot weep, yet give some groans,
   Though not for me, yet for your aching bones.

50   Brethren and sisters of the hold-door trade,
   Some two months hence my will shall here be made.
   It should be now, but that my fear is this,

53   Some gallèd goose of Winchester would hiss.

54   Till then I'll sweat and seek about for eases,
   And at that time bequeath you my diseases.'   *[Exit.]*

---

45 *painted cloths* painted cloth hangings (used like tapestries, and sometimes to advertise wares) **50** *hold-door trade* prostitution **53** *gallèd
goose* irritated prostitute; *Winchester* (the brothels of Southwark had
once been under the jurisdiction of the Bishop of Winchester, a prostitute
being called a Winchester goose) **54** *sweat* (a treatment for venereal
diseases)

APPENDIX:
THE QUARTO AND FOLIO TEXTS

As indicated in the "Note on the text", both the quarto and folio texts have substantive value. In addition to the passages bracketed, a number of readings in the present text have been adopted from the folio. These are noted below, along with all other material departures from the quarto text. The adopted reading in italics is followed by the quarto reading in roman.

Preface   17 *witted* wittied   30 *judgment's* Iudgements   36 *state* states

Pro. (supplied from F) 8 *immures* emures   12 *barks* barke   19 *Sperr* Stirre

I, i, 23 *of* (F) Omitted (Q)   25 *you* (F) yea   *to* (F) Omitted (Q)   39 *An* And   50 *Pour'st* (F) Powrest   64 *an* And   67–68 *ill-thought-on* (F) ill thought   72 *An* and   *not* (F) Omitted (Q)   73 *on* (F) a   *care* (F) Omitted (Q)   74 *an* and   92 *tetchy* teachy

I, ii, 17 *they* (F) the   43 *Ilium* (F) Illum   46 *ye* yea   82 *wit* will   111 *lift* (F) liste   120 *an* and   123 *the* thee   145 *An't* And t'   181 *a* (F) Omitted (Q)   193 *man's* (F) man   199 *anything;* anything   *an* and   200 s.d. (after l. 198 in Q)   211–12 *indifferent well.* indifferent, well,   275 *prize* (F) price

I, iii, 2 *the jaundice on* the Iaundies on (F) these Iaundies ore (Q)   13 *every* (F) ever   31 *thy* (F) the   36 *patient* (F) ancient   54 *Returns* Retires   56 *spirit* (F) spright   61 *thy* (F) the   72 *lips than* lips; then   75 *basis* (F) bases   87 *Insisture* (F) In sisture   110 *meets* (F) melts   156 *scaffoldage* scoaffollage   157 *o'er-wrested* ore-rested   159 *unsquared* (F) unsquare   179 *natures,* (F) natures   188 *self-willed* (F) selfe-wild   195 *and* (F) our   209 *fineness* (F) finesse   212 s.d. (F) Omitted (Q)   214 s.d. (F) Omitted (Q)   238 *Jove's* (F) great Ioves   247 *affair* (F) affaires   250 *him* (F) with him   252 *the* (F) that   256 *loud* (F) alowd

262 *this* (F) his   263 *rusty* (F) restie   267 *That seeks* (F) And feeds   276 *compass* (F) couple   289 *or means* (F) a meanes   294 *one* (F) no   297 *vantbrace* (F) vambrace   *this withered brawn* (F) my withered braunes   298 *will* (F) Omitted (Q)   302 *youth* (F) men   304 *Agamemnon* (F) Omitted (Q)   305 *first* (F) sir   327 *Achilles, were* (F) Achilles weare   334 *his honor* (F) those honours   336 *this* (F) the   354 *his* in his   369 *we* (F) it   372 *did* (F) do   390 *tarre* (F) arre

II, i, 13 *vinewed'st* whinid'st (F) unsalted (Q)   16 *oration* (F) oration without booke   17 *a* (F) Omitted (Q)   18 *murrain* murren (F) murrion (Q)   *o' ath*   25 *an* and   36, 38, 39 *Thersites, Ajax, Thersites* (F) Omitted (Q)   43 *Thou* (F) you   67 *I* (F) It   71 *I'll* (F) I   92 *sufferance* (F) suffrance   97 *if he* (F) and out (F) at   101 *your* their   *on their toes* (F) Omitted (Q)   109 *brach* brooch   117 *fifth* (F) first

II, ii, 14, 15 *surety* (F) surely   17 *worst.* (F) worst   27 *father* (F) fathers   33 *at* (F) of   47 *Let's* (F) Sets   64 *shores* (F) shore   79 *stale* (F) pale   82 *launched* (F) lansh't   100 s.d. (after l. 96 in Q)   210 *strike* (F) shrike

II, iii, 1 *Thersites* [s.p.] (F) Omitted (Q)   20 s.d. (F) Omitted (Q)   24 *wouldst* (F) couldst   29 *art* (F) art not   30 *corse* course   45 *thyself* (F) Thersites   59 *of Agamemnon* (F) Omitted (Q)   63 *Creator* (F) Prover   66 s.d. (F) Omitted (Q)   75 *shent* sent (F) sate (Q)   79 *so say* (F) say so   110 *winged* wingèd   126 *as* (F) and   127 *carriage of this action* (F) streame of his commencement   137 *enter you* (F) entertaine   156 s.d. (after l. 153 in Q)   187 *titled* (F) liked   197 *pash* (F) push   199 *An* and   206 *let* (F) tell   209, 213 *An* And   214 *Ulysses* (F) Aiax   215 *Ajax* (F) Omitted (Q)   216 *Nestor* (after *warm* in l. 216 in Q)   217 *praises* (F) praiers *pour in, pour in* (F) poure in, poure   234 *got* (F) gat   236 *all* (F) all thy   242 *bourn* (F) boord   243 *Thy* (F) This   257 *cull* (F) call

III, i, 6 *noble* (F) notable   24 *friend* (F) Omitted (Q)   34 *you not* (F) not you   36 *that* (F) Omitted (Q)   87 *poor* (F) Omitted (Q)   99 *lord* (F) lad   109 *shaft confounds* (F) shafts confound   140 *these* (F) this   148 *thee* (F) her

III, ii, 3 *he* (F) Omitted (Q)   8 *a* to a   10 *those* (F) these   42, 45 *an* and   63 *fears* teares   75 *is* (F) Omitted (Q)   86 *crown it. No perfection* (F) lover part no affection   92 s.d. (F) Omitted (Q)   111 *glance that ever* – glance ; that ever   113 *not, till now* (F) till now not   125 *Cunning* Comming   134 *An* and   149 *might ;*

might   152 *aye* (F) age   159 *winnowed* winnowèd   168 *similes,*
(F) simele's   172 *Yet* (F) Omitted (Q)   177 *and* (F) or   185 *as*
(F) or   192 *pains* (F) paine

III, iii 33 *his* this   39 *to* (F) Omitted (Q)   44 *med'cinable* medecin-
able   102 *giver* (F) givers   119 *th'* (F) the   128 *abject* (F)
obiect   140 *on* (F) one   141 *shrinking* (F) shriking   155 *one*
(F) on   158 *hedge* (F) turne   160 *hindmost;* (F) him, most,
162 *rear* neere   164 *past* (F) passe   177 *give* goe   197 *grain of
Pluto's gold* (F) thing   198 *th'* (F) the   *deeps* (F) depth   200
Does Do   224 *a* (F) Omitted (Q)   233 *we* (F) they   255 *an* and
265 *to him* (F) Omitted (Q)   272 *most* (F) Omitted (Q)   276
Grecian (F) Omitted (Q)   *et caetera* (F) Omitted (Q)   288 *be
wi'* buy

IV, i, s.d. *with a torch* (F) Omitted (Q)   4 *you* (F) your   15 *and, so
long,* and so long   16 *But* (F) Lul'd   40 *do think* (F) beleeve
52 *the* (F) Omitted (Q)   56 *soilure* (F) soyle   76 *you* (F) they

IV, ii, 6 *infants'* infants   22 s.d. (F) Omitted (Q)   31 *capocchia*
chipochia   51 *'Tis* (F) its   63 *us* (F) him   *for him* (F) Omitted
(Q)   66 *concluded so* (F) so concluded   72 *nature* (F) neighbor
Pandar   77 *Cressida* (F) Omitted (Q)

IV, iv, 4 *as* (F) is   53 *the root* (F) my throate   63 *there's* (F) there is
76 *They're* Their   78 *person* (F) portion   134 *I'll* (F) I   138 s.d.
Sound trumpet (F) Omitted (Q)

IV, v, 95 *Agamemnon* (F) Ulisses [not a s.p.]   97 *matchless,* (F)
matchlesse   98 *in deeds* (F) deeds   115 *disposed* (F) dispo'd
132 *drop* (F) day   142 *O yes* O yes   160 *mine* (F) my   177 *that I
affect th' untraded oath* (F) thy affect, the untraded earth   187
thy (F) th'   192 *shraped* shrupd   198 *Let* (F) O let   234 *prithee*
(F) pray thee   254 *stithied* (F) stichied   283 *thee* (F) you   286
As (F) But   291 *she loved* (F) my Lord

V, i, 12 *need these* (F) needs this   14 *boy* (F) box   17 *catarrhs* (F)
Omitted (Q)   18 *o' a*   19 *wheezing* whissing   20 *lime-kilns*
lime-kills   21–22 *and the like* (F) Omitted (Q)   31 *tassel* (F)
toslell   32 *pestered* pestred   37 *in to-morrow's* (F) into mor-
rowes   46 s.d. (F) Omitted (Q)   52 *brother* (F) be   54 *hanging*
(F) Omitted (Q)   55 *brother's* (F) bare   56 *forced* (F) faced   58
he is (F) her's   *dog* (F) day   59 *mule* (F) Moyle   *fitchew* (F)
Fichooke   61 *Menelaus!* Menelaus   *not* (F) Omitted (Q)   64
spirits (F) sprites   75 *sewer* sure   76 *at once* (F) Omitted (Q)
97 s.d. *Exit* Exeunt (F) Omitted (Q)

V, ii, 5 s.d. (F) Omitted (Q)   13 *Cressida.* Cal.   34 *you* (F) Omitted

(Q) 38 *Nay* (F) Now   39 *distraction* (F) distruction   44 *withered* witherèd   45 *Why, Greek!* why Greeke?   46 *adieu* (F) Omitted (Q)   54 *these* (F) Omitted (Q)   55 *But* (F) Omitted (Q)   56 *la* lo   66 *Cressida* (F) Troy: 68 *have't* (F) ha't   74 *in* (F) on   77 *Nay* Dio: [s.p.] Nay   78 *He* Cres: [s.p.] He   81 *Cressida* (F) Omitted (Q)   85 *one's* on's   87 *By* (F) And by   100 *Ay,* (F) I   101 *plagued* (F) plaguèd   110 *say* (F) said   114 *co-act* (F) Court   119 *had deceptious* (F) were deceptions   130 *soil* (F) spoile   147 *orifice* orifex   148 *Ariachne's* (F) Ariachna's   153 *five-* (F) finde   156 *bound* (F) given   163 *as I* I

V, iii, 14 *Cassandra* (F) Cres.   21 *give* count give   *use* as   29 *mean'st* (F) meanest   39 *that, good Troilus?* that? good Troylus   85 *distraction* (F) destruction   104 *o' these* ath's

V, iv, 3 *young* (F) Omitted (Q)   15 *begin* began   25 *art thou* (F) art

V, v, 22 *scalèd* (F) scaling   41 *luck* (F) lust   43 *Ajax* (F) Omitted (Q)

V, vi, 1 *Ajax* (F) Omitted (Q)   2 *Diomedes* (F) Omitted (Q)   13 *Achilles* (F) Omitted (Q)   *thee* thee ha   26 *reck* wreake   *thou* (F) I

V, vii, 1 *Achilles* (F) Omitted (Q)   10 *'Loo* lowe   *'loo* lowe   11 *-horned* hen'd   *'Loo, Paris, 'loo* lowe Paris, lowe   12 s.d. *Exeunt* Exit   16 *am a bastard* (F) am bastard

V, viii, 4 s.d. *his* (F) Omitted (Q)   15 *part* (F) prat   16 *Greek* (F) One   *Troyan trumpets* (F) Troyans trumpet

V, ix, 1 *shout is that* (F) is this

V, x, s.d. *and* (F) Omitted (Q)   3 *Troilus* (F) before l. 2 in Q   8 *say,* say   12 *fear, of* (F) feare of   17 *there* (F) their   23 *vile* (F) proud   24 *pight* (F) pitcht   29 *frenzy's* (F) frienzes   33 *broker lackey!* broker, lacky,   *Ignomy and* (F) ignomyny   49 *your* (F) my

The Complete Pelican
SHAKESPEARE

To fill the need for a convenient and authoritative one-volume edition, the thirty-eight books in the Pelican series have been brought together.

THE COMPLETE PELICAN SHAKESPEARE includes all the material contained in the separate volumes, together with a 50,000-word General Introduction and full bibliographies. It contains the first nineteen pages of the First Folio in reduced facsimile, five new drawings, and illustrated endpapers.

$9\frac{3}{4} \times 7\frac{3}{16}$ inches, 1520 pages
Trade Edition cloth-bound, in jacket and slipcase
Text Edition cloth-bound

PENGUIN SHAKESPEARE LIBRARY

General Editor: Professor T. J. B. Spencer
Director of the Shakespeare Institute, University of Birmingham

A new series of reprints of critical works, source-books, and other aids to the understanding of Shakespeare